Twayne's United States Authors Series

EDITOR OF THIS VOLUME

Warren French
Indiana University

Joan Didion

TUSAS 370

Joan Didion

JOAN DIDION

By MARK ROYDEN WINCHELL

TWAYNE PUBLISHERS
A DIVISION OF G. K. HALL & CO., BOSTON

Printed on permanent/durable acid-free paper and bound
in the United States of America

First Printing

Frontispiece photo of Joan Didion
by Mary Lloyd Estrin

Library of Congress Cataloging in Publication Data

Winchell, Mark Royden, 1948–
Joan Didion.

(Twayne's United States authors series; TUSAS 370)
Bibliography: p. 172–175
Includes index.
1. Didion, Joan—Criticism and interpretation.
PS3554.I33Z95   818'.5409   80–10553
ISBN 0–8057–7308–8

To my parents, John and Gertrude Winchell,
To my aunt, Mrs. Pauline Richardson Cordes, and
To the memory of my grandmother, Mrs. Elbert Settle,
This book is lovingly dedicated.

Contents

About the Author

Born in 1948, Mark Royden Winchell is a native of Columbus, Ohio. He received his B.A. and M.A. degrees in English from West Virginia University in 1971 and 1973, respectively, and his Ph.D. in English from Vanderbilt University in 1978. His work has appeared in the *Sewanee Review*, the *Mississippi Quarterly*, *Christianity and Literature*, and the *West Virginia University Philological Papers*. Moreover, he has contributed to three books: *Contemporary Literary Criticism*, Vol. 13, the third edition of William Rose Benet's *Reader's Encyclopedia*, and *The Literature of Tennessee*. At present he is revising his doctoral dissertation—*One Foot in Paradise: The American Adam in the Modern World*—for publication. Other projects in the works include a critical book on the writings of William F. Buckley, Jr., and a monograph on Horace McCoy. In addition to his parents, Mr. Winchell's immediate family includes a brother and sister-in-law—Timothy and Margaret Hull Winchell of Dayton, Ohio.

Preface

Although Joan Didion is one of our most important contemporary writers, she has yet to be the focus of an extended critical study. On the whole, serious students of Didion's work must content themselves with cursory book reviews and with ephemeral biographical features in personality-oriented journals. These writings may provide one with interesting glimpses of *parts* of their subject's career, but clearly there is a need to see the larger shape of that career and to evaluate the contribution which Didion has made to recent American letters. The following study is meant to be a response to that need.

The first six and a half chapters of this book focus on Didion's nonfiction prose. Although much of that prose has been collected in *Slouching Towards Bethlehem* (1968) and *The White Album* (1979), I have also included in my discussion a number of significant essays which are available only in old issues of such magazines as *Vogue*, *National Review*, *Saturday Evening Post*, and *Life*. Furthermore, in approaching the total body of Didion's journalism I have been less interested in the chronological order in which particular essays have appeared or in the format in which they have been preserved than in certain basic thematic patterns which run through those essays. (Indeed, considering our unavoidable lack of historical perspective on a writer so current as Didion, it makes better critical sense to identify important characteristics of her thought and style than to attempt "definitive" judgments about which of her writings will survive and which will fade from memory. For this reason I have sought to be comprehensive rather than selective in my consideration of the author's expository prose.)

The bulk of Chapters 7 and 9 and all of Chapters 8 and 10 deal with Didion's fiction—her three novels and four published short stories. By saving her fiction until last, we are able to view it in light of its author's essays. This is not to say that the essays serve only as a gloss on the fiction—Didion has created genuine works of art in *both* genres—but rather that many of the attitudes and preoccupations which obliquely inform her novels and stories are rendered more directly in her nonfiction prose. Thus, by working our way from her journalism to her more purely imaginative works, we can gain an incremental understanding of the craft and vision of Joan Didion, a major presence in contemporary American writing.

MARK ROYDEN WINCHELL

Acknowledgments

I am pleased to acknowledge certain individuals without whose valued assistance this book would not have appeared in its present form. To begin with, I thank Miss Joan Didion for answering several questions by mail, for correcting some factual inaccuracies in the original version of my biographical chapter, and for granting me permission to quote from her copyrighted work. I am also indebted to Wayne Batten, Lloyd Davis, Paul Reeve, Gregory Schirmer, Victor Strandberg, and Walter Sullivan for reading and commenting on parts of this book.

Among those persons who aided me in securing needed resources I am particularly grateful to Margaret Greenlee and William Pollard of Belmont College; to Richard Fulk and James Sandlin of the Office of Student Services, Vanderbilt University; and to Miss Didion's agent Lois Wallace. Moreover, I thank my parents for providing me with material support and moral encouragement in this endeavor.

In addition to reading parts of this book, Professor Thomas Daniel Young has extended its author perceptive guidance and generous counsel on occasions too numerous to mention.

Finally, I owe a special debt of thanks to James Calland and to Warren French for reading the entire book many times and in many forms. One is indeed fortunate to have an editor with the patience and insight of Professor French. Working with him has been both an education and a pleasure.

The author also wishes to thank the publishers and holders of copyright named below for permission to use quotations:

Selections from *Play it as it Lays* by Joan Didion. Copyright © 1970 by Joan Didion. Selections from "Slouching Towards Bethlehem" by Joan Didion. Copyright © 1961, 1964, 1965, 1967, 1968 by Joan Didion. Reprinted with the permission of Farrar, Straus and Giroux, Inc.

Selections from *The White Album* by Joan Didion. Copyright © 1979 by Joan Didion. Selections from *A Book of Common Prayer* by Joan Didion. Copyright © 1977 by Joan Didion. Reprinted by per-

Chronology

1934   Joan Didion born in Sacramento, California, December 5, daughter of Frank (Reese) and Eduene (Jerrett) Didion.

1952   Graduates from C. K. McClatchy High School in Sacramento.

1953   Enters the University of California at Berkeley in February.

1956   Graduates from Berkeley; publishes first story—"Sunset"—in student literary magazine *Occident*; wins Vogue's *Prix de Paris* award.

1956–   Lives in New York; writes for *Vogue, Mademoiselle*, and
1964   *National Review.*

1963   *Run River*

1964   Marries John Gregory Dunne in January; moves back to California in June; short story "Coming Home" (*Saturday Evening Post*).

1964–   Writes regular movie column for *Vogue*; publishes essays in
1966   *Holiday, Saturday Evening Post, New York Times Magazine*, and *American Scholar.*

1965   Short story "The Welfare Island Ferry" (*Harper's Bazaar*).

1966   Adopts infant daughter Quintana.

1967   Short story "When Did Music Come This Way? Children Dear, Was It Yesterday?" (*Denver Quarterly*).

1967–   With Dunne shares "Points West" column in *Saturday*
1969   *Evening Post.*

1968   *Slouching Towards Bethlehem.*

1969–   Writes column for *Life.*
1970

1970   *Play It as It Lays.*

1971   *The Panic in Needle Park* (film).

1972   Film version of *Play It as It Lays.*

1972–   Publishes in *New York Times Book Review, New York*
1979   *Review of Books*, and *Esquire.*

1975   Serves as Regents Lecturer, University of California at Berkeley.

1976–   With Dunne shares "The Coast" column in *Esquire.*
1977

1977 *A Book of Common Prayer.*
1979 *The White Album.*

CHAPTER 1

Notes on the Native Daughter

IN 1964 Joan Didion described herself as being "in my late twenties, a relatively articulate member of the most inarticulate segment of the middle class, the kind of woman who sets store by her great-grandmother's orange spoons, by well-mannered children, by the avoidance of chic and by a sense of sin."[1] Accordingly, we find in her writings—three novels, two volumes of essays, and a considerable body of uncollected prose—the sort of complex perspective which enables us to see—in addition to the shape and texture of those orange spoons—that world of the spirit in which a sense of sin resides.

In possessing this doubleness of vision, however, Didion is not unique; rather, she joins company with the best literary artists of the ages. For such artists manage to suffuse their works with a luminous, prismatic quality not unlike that of a china night lamp Eudora Welty remembers from her childhood: "The outside is painted with a scene, which is one thing; then, when the lamp is lighted, through the porcelain sides a new picture comes out through the old and they are seen as one. . . . The lamp alight is the combination of internal and external, glowing at the imagination as one; and so is the good novel. Seeing that these inner and outer surfaces do lie so close together and so implicit in each other, the wonder is that human life so often separates them, or appears to, and it takes a good novel to put them back together."[2]

Clearly, Joan Didion is the "kind of woman" who can turn on the night lamp of the imagination. Why this is so is properly the concern of the biographer; how it is so, of the literary critic. In approaching Didion, however, one finds that the roles of biographer and literary critic occasionally overlap. This is because she has written a number of fine autobiographical essays; and to the extent that we concern ourselves with these essays, we must also concern ourselves with the way in which her life has become a source for her art. In doing this it is perhaps best to begin with her essay "On Keeping a Notebook," for here, Didion comments very explicitly on the relationship between personal experience and literary art.

To begin with she makes it clear that keeping a notebook differs from keeping a diary: in a diary the day's events are factually recorded; in a notebook they are imaginatively reconstituted. Expressing her preference for the latter activity and for the theory of knowledge it implies, Didion writes:

Not only have I always had trouble distinguishing between what happened and what merely might have happened, but I remain unconvinced that the distinction, for my purposes, matters. The cracked crab I recall having for lunch the day my father came home from Detroit in 1945 must certainly be embroidery, worked into the day's pattern to lend verisimilitude. . . . And yet it is precisely that fictitious crab that makes me see the afternoon all over again, a home movie run all too often, the father bearing gifts, the children weeping, an exercise in family love and guilt. Or that is what it was to me. Similarly, perhaps it never did snow that August in Vermont; perhaps there never were flurries in the night wind, and maybe no one else felt the ground hardening and the summer already dead even as we pretended to bask in it, but that was how it felt to me, and it might as well have snowed, could have snowed, did snow. (p. 134)[3]

Didion's writing is filled with aesthetic equivalents of cracked crab and snow in Vermont. Speaking in another context and of another writer—Graham Greene—she calls such things "marks of identity."[4] Indeed, at one level writing may well be a kind of search for identity, an attempt to create an ideal *persona*, to bestow artistic coherence upon the randomness of life. (In a sense the very notion of identity is itself an artistic construct; for raw experience is a constant state of flux shaped only by the perceiving consciousness.) Thus Didion is striving through the written word for what most of us strive for in a somewhat less deliberate and less verbal form—self-knowledge. She thinks "we are well advised to keep on nodding terms with the people we used to be, whether we find them attractive company or not. Otherwise they turn up unannounced and surprise us, come hammering on the mind's door at 4 a.m. of a bad night and demand to know who deserted them, who betrayed them, who is going to make amends." "We forget all too soon the things we thought we could never forget," she tells us. "We forget the loves and the betrayals alike, forget what we whispered and what we screamed, forget who we were" (*Slouching*, p. 139).

I   *The Artist as a Young Woman*

Although Didion has written very little about the first twenty years of her life, it is possible to piece together some information concerning her childhood. We know, for example, that she was born in Sacramento, California on December 5, 1934, to Frank (Reese) and Eduene (Jerrett) Didion. We also know that her sense of identity as a daughter of California's Central Valley has profoundly affected her moral and aesthetic sensibility. Since her great-great-great-grandmother Nancy Hardin Cornwall came west on a wagon train in 1846, Didion is—in fact—a fifth-generation Californian. She carries the heritage of the frontier in her genes and with it a sense of life's very contingency. (Indeed, Nancy Hardin Cornwall came most of the way west with the Donner-Reed Party, only cutting north to Oregon at Humboldt Sink; and Mrs. Cornwall's historically conscious descendant admits even today to being "haunted by the cannibalism of the Donner Party."[5])

Didion's California childhood was itself interrupted by the contingency of history when—two days after her seventh birthday—the Japanese attacked Pearl Harbor, an event which "meant war and my father going away and makeshift Christmases in rented rooms near Air Corps bases and nothing the same ever again" (*Slouching*, p. 189). But with the end of the war came a return to Sacramento and an adolescence which coincided with the expansive optimism of America in the late 1940s. The author remembers with particular vividness the summers of those years. "Because my own middle childhood was spent in the Sacramento Valley," she writes, "where summer is less a season than a five-month siege, my mother and brother and I would go, come June, to a place on the Marin County coast called Stinson Beach: unkempt, desolate, so rickety that geraniums obscured even the sunbleached Coca-Cola signs. . . . At Stinson Beach, the raciest available diversion was playing 'Ghost Riders in the Sky' on the jukebox in the combination grocery store, drugstore, and Greyhound bus station. (I recall, flawlessly, the social high spot of my eleventh summer: a day's excursion to San Francisco to have my chest X-rayed.)"[6]

At fourteen, however, the social high spot of her year may well have been her initiation into a high school sorority called the Mañana Club. Since Nina Warren—daughter of California governor Earl Warren and a fellow student with Didion at C. K. McClatchy High—was a prominent member of that club, the initiation was held in the old California governor's mansion—a house which still commands a special place in the author's affections.[7]

Although Didion must have suffered her share of adolescent traumata, her only published account of one is found in her April 6, 1968, *Saturday Evening Post* column, "On Being Unchosen by the College of One's Choice." Here, she tells of the rejection of her application to Stanford. The mimeographed letter informing her of that rejection began "Dear Joan"—although the writer did not know her at all—and was signed Rixford K. Snyder, Director of Admissions. Didion describes her anguished reaction:

I remember quite clearly the afternoon I opened that letter. . . . For a while I sat on the floor of my closet and buried my face in an old quilted robe and later, after the situation's real humiliations (all my friends who applied to Stanford had been admitted) had faded into safe theatrics, I sat on the edge of the bathtub and thought about swallowing the contents of an old bottle of codeine-and-Empirin. I saw myself in an oxygen tent, with Rixford K. Snyder hovering outside, although how the news was to reach Rixford K. Snyder was a plot point that troubled me even as I counted out the tablets.

She did not take the pills, however. Instead, "I spent the rest of the spring in sullen but mild rebellion, sitting around drive-ins, listening to Tulsa evangelists on the car radio, and in the summer I fell in love with someone who wanted to be a golf pro, and I spent a lot of time watching him practice putting, and in the fall I went to a junior college a couple of hours a day and made up the credits I needed to go to the University of California at Berkeley."[8]

Today when we think of Berkeley, we are apt to remember the Berkeley of the 1960s. A national metonymy for student radicalism, it was first the home of Mario Savio and the free speech movement and later of Vietnam Day protests against the American war in Indochina. The Berkeley of Joan Didion's undergraduate days, however, was a vastly different place. In a selection from *The White Album* entitled "On the Morning After the Sixties" she writes: "We were that generation called 'silent,' but we were silent neither, as some thought, because we shared the period's official optimism nor, as others thought, because we feared its official repression. We were silent because the exhilaration of social action seemed to many of us just one more way of escaping the personal, of masking for a while that dread of the meaningless which was man's fate" (pp. 206–207).[9]

The scene with which this essay opens establishes an atmosphere which is quintessentially of the 1950s. Here, the author lies on a leather couch in a fraternity house, reading a book by Lionel Trilling and listening to a middle-aged man try vainly to pick out the melodic line to "Blue Room" on a piano. "I can hear and see it still," she writes, "the wrong note in 'We will thrive on/Keep alive on,' the sunlight falling through the big windows, the man picking up his drink and beginning again and telling me, without ever saying a word, something I had not known before about bad marriages and wasted time and looking backward" (p. 205).

There are other memories from that era, memories of "certain small things" which like Wordsworthian spots of time punctuated the prevailing depression and ennui of young adulthood. She remembers "a woman picking daffodils in the rain one day when I was walking in the hills . . . , a teacher who drank too much one night and revealed his fright and bitterness . . . , my real joy at discovering for the first time how language worked, at discovering, for example, that the central line of *Heart of Darkness* was a postscript" (p. 207).

During her junior and senior years Didion lived by herself in a large bare apartment—"(I had lived a while in a sorority, the Tri Delt House, and had left it, typically, not over any 'issue' but because I, the implacable 'I,' did not like living with sixty people)"—and there she read Camus, Orwell, and Henry James. "I watched a flowering plum come in and out of blossom," she tells us, "and at night, most nights, I walked outside and looked up to where the cyclotron and the bevatron glowed on the dark hillside, unspeakable mysteries which engaged me, in the style of my time, only personally." Summing up her later experience, she writes: "I got out of Berkeley and went to New York and later I got out of New York and came to Los Angeles. What I have made for myself is personal, but is not exactly peace" (pp. 207–208).

In 1956 Joan Didion was graduated from Berkeley and won *Vogue's Prix de Paris* contest. She lived for the next eight years in New York writing for *National Review* and for *Mademoiselle*, as well as for *Vogue* itself.[10] Also, during these years she appeared for three consecutive nights on a TV quiz show called "Crosswits,"[11] published her first novel, *Run River*, and—after seven year's acquaintance—married a young Irishman from Connecticut named John Gregory Dunne.[12] However, in the definitive essay on her years in New York—"Goodbye to All That" (*Slouching*, pp. 225–38)—she concentrates less on the facts of her experience than on its emotional character. She gives us what is, in effect, a personal essay in the tradition of William Hazlitt, Charles Lamb, and Robert Louis Stevenson.

The tone which the author maintains here is basically elegiac. New York was for Didion at one time an enchanted city (indeed, the original title of this essay was "Farewell to the Enchanted City") and something of the magic which New York held for her comes across in passages of lyrical intensity. She loved New York "the way you love the first person who ever touches you and never love anyone quite that way again" (p. 228). She writes: "I remember walking across Sixty-second Street one twilight that first spring, or the second spring, they were all alike for a while. I was late to meet someone but I stopped at Lexington Avenue and bought a peach and stood on the corner eating it and knew that I had come out of the West and reached the mirage" (p. 228).

In Chapter 7 we will look at the mythic significance for Didion's writing of the journey to the West. What we have in "Goodbye to All That," however, is the opposite of that journey. (Indeed, Didion's migration from California to New York is not unlike that of a Henry James heroine from the New World to Europe, or—for that matter— of a Nick Carraway from the Midwest to Long Island.) To her mind she had come to make her way in what we know of civilization "where Wall Street and Fifth Avenue and Madison Avenue were not places at all but abstractions ('Money,' and 'High Fashion,' and 'The Hucksters')." "New York was no mere city," she tells us. "It was instead an infinitely romantic notion, the mysterious nexus of all love and money and power, the shining and perishable dream itself. To think of 'living' there was to reduce the miraculous to the mundane; one does not 'live' at Xanadu" (p. 231).

The nursery rhyme which serves as an epigraph to this essay is itself suggestive. It reads:

> How many miles to Babylon?
> Three score miles and ten—
> Can I get there by candlelight?
> Yes, and back again—
> If your feet are nimble and light
> You can get there by candlelight.

In commenting on this rhyme Iona and Peter Opie point out that two interpretations are most frequently advanced for the term "Babylon." One holds that that term is actually a corruption of "Babyland"; while the more accepted view sees Babylon as "the far-away luxurious city of seventeenth-century usage."[13] In a sense both interpretations may be applicable here. For Didion New York is at once a "far-away luxurious city" and a town "for only the very young" (p. 227). ("Part of what I want to tell you is what it is like to be young in New York, how six months can become eight years with the deceptive ease of a film dissolve, for that is how those years appear to me now, in a long sequence of sentimental dissolves and old-fashioned trick shots—the Seagram Building fountains dissolve into snowflakes, I enter a revolving door at twenty and come out a good deal older, and on a different street," p. 227).

Essentially, this essay is an act of memory. The author's double focus is continually emphasized by such phrases as "I remember," and "In retrospect it seems to me," and by her wistful but perceptive analysis of the ingenuous young woman she used to be. She tells us, for example, of her first three days in New York when she lay "wrapped in blankets in a hotel room air-conditioned to 35° and tried to get over a bad cold and a high fever" (p. 226). She didn't call a doctor because she knew no doctors and she didn't call anyone to turn down the air conditioner because she didn't know how much to tip whoever might come. "Was anyone ever so young?" she asks. "I am here to tell you that someone was" (p. 227). According to Didion, youth is not just a time of life but a state of delusion—a delusion that the emotional costs which we incur in life need never be paid or can be indefinitely deferred. When those costs began coming due for her, her youth was over. And so too was the enchantment of Babylon.

The structure of "Goodbye to All That" is neither thematic nor chronological so much as it is impressionistic. Whether Didion is enthralled by her environment—as she was during her early years in New York—or palpably oppressed by it—as she was to become later on—her relationship with that environment seems so nearly unique as to be virtually solipsistic ("one of the mixed blessings of being twenty and twenty-one and even twenty-three is the conviction that nothing like this, all evidence to the contrary notwithstanding, has ever happened to anyone before," p. 226). Her essay is replete with names of places, but other people are almost never named. (We know that her husband used to take her to Michael's Pub and to Toots Shor's for dinner; but we don't know who her husband is, how she met him, or much about their life together.) When other people do appear it is in vague, generic terms: she talks of "a friend who complained of having been around too long" (pp. 227–28), of "someone who did have the West Village number" (p. 235), of people who "had moved to Dallas or had gone on Antabuse or had bought a farm in New Hampshire" (p. 238). No, real people don't live in the mirage, Didion seems to be saying. But some come to painful maturity just passing through.

II   *The Ties That Bind*

Joan Didion and John Gregory Dunne were married in January 1964 and that June returned to California to live. Didion continued writing for *National Review* and for *Vogue* (contributing among other things a regular movie column to the latter) and also published in such diverse periodicals as *Holiday*, the *Saturday Evening Post*, the *New York Times Magazine*, and the *American Scholar*. From June 1967 to January 1969 she and Dunne were responsible for a *Saturday Evening Post* column called "Points West"—each of them writing in alternate issues—and in 1968 a selection of Didion's essays was published under the title *Slouching Towards Bethlehem*. Moreover, their personal lives were dramatically altered when—in 1966—the Dunnes adopted an infant daughter they named Quintana Roo.[14]

In her essay "On Going Home" (*Slouching*, pp. 164–68) Didion writes about returning to Sacramento for Quintana's first birthday. She tells us that when she returns to the Central Valley she invariably falls into the insular ways of her family, ways which mean little to her husband. "We live in dusty houses," she writes, "filled with mementos quite without value to him (what could the Canton dessert plates mean to him? how could he have known about the assay scales, why should he care if he did know?), and we appear to talk exclusively about people we know who have been committed to mental hospitals, about people we know who have been booked on drunk-driving charges, and about property, particularly about property, land, price per acre and C-2 zoning and assessments and freeway access" (p. 164). What Dunne does not realize is that when Didion and her family talk about these things, they are actually "talking in code about the things we like best, the yellow fields and the cottonwoods and the rivers rising and falling and the mountain roads closing when the heavy snow comes in" (p. 165).

For Didion the concept of home is in a sense temporal as well as spatial. "Sometimes I think that those of us who are now in our thirties," she writes, "were born into the last generation to carry the burden of 'home,' to find in family life the source of all tension and drama." She continues:

The question of whether or not you could go home again was a very real part of the sentimental and largely literary baggage with which we left home in the fifties; I suspect that it is irrelevant to the children born of the fragmentation after World War II. A few weeks ago in a San Francisco bar I saw a pretty young girl on crystal take off her clothes and dance for the cash prize in an "amateur-topless" contest. There was no particular sense of moment about this, none of the effect of romantic degradation, of "dark journey," for which my generation strived so assiduously. What sense could that girl possibly make of, say, *Long Day's Journey into Night*? Who is beside the point? (pp. 165–66)

It is perhaps ironically fitting that an essay so insistently about the demands of the past should be occasioned by the birthday of a one-year-old child. If the life which that child's mother knew as a girl is gone, and if home itself has become an antiquated notion, what can the author promise to her daughter? "I would like to promise her," Didion writes, "that she will grow up with a sense of her cousins and of rivers and of her great-grandmother's teacups, would like to pledge her a picnic on a river with fried chicken and her hair uncombed, would like to give her *home* for her birthday, but we live differently now and I can promise her nothing like that. I give her a xylophone and a sundress from Madeira, and promise to tell her a funny story" (pp. 167–68).

Unfortunately, it would be wrong to assume that because Didion's present life is different from the one which she knew as a child that she has simply found a new kind of "home." Instead, she is—in a very real sense—cast adrift in the modern world. Indeed, the title of her December 5, 1969, *Life* column, "A Problem of Making Connections," could apply with equal validity to much of her autobiographical writing. With painful honesty she describes the emotionally fragmented and spiritually desensitized life she leads. "I remember leaving someone once," she writes, "a long time ago, one bad afternoon in New York, packing a suitcase and crying while he watched me. When I asked him finally how he could watch me, he told me that a great many things had happened to him during the 10 years before I knew him, and nothing much touched him anymore. I remember saying that I never wanted to get the way he was, and he looked at me a long while before he answered. 'Nobody wants to,' he said. 'But you will.'"[15]

The tone of this essay is direct and immediate: Didion addresses the reader as "you" and employs the present tense. She tells us that she is at the Royal Hawaiian Hotel in Honolulu with her husband and daughter during a time of personal crisis. Although the precise nature of this crisis is never specified, one gathers that the author's marriage is experiencing considerable stress. (We see her with Dunne and Quintana sitting in their hotel room awaiting news of a possible tidal wave: "The bulletin, when it comes, is a distinct anticlimax: Midway reports no unusual wave action. My husband switches off the TV set and stares out the window. I avoid his eyes and brush the baby's hair. In the absence of a natural disaster we are left again to our own uneasy devices. We are here on this island in the middle of the Pacific in lieu of filing for divorce.") What is significant here, however, are not the details of Didion's personal life—details which she wisely spares us—but her ability to apprehend the chaos which surrounds her and, in so doing, somehow to transcend it.

We hear an echo of Prufrock's declaration, "I am not Prince

Hamlet," in Didion's statement, "I am not the society in microcosm"; however, like Prufrock Didion is only partially correct. Although her perspective is uniquely her own, it is not without some subterranean reference to life beyond her immediate situation, "to the stuff of bad dreams, the children burning in the locked car in the supermarket parking lot, the bike boys stripping down stolen cars on the captive cripple's ranch, the freeway sniper who feels 'real bad' about picking off the family of five, the hustlers, the insane, the cunning Okie faces that turn up in military investigations, the sullen lurkers in doorways, the lost children, all the ignorant armies on some dark pathological plain." I think that we can concur with James McGrath of New York City who writes to the editor of *Life*: Joan Didion "is not your average housewife worrying about stubborn stains on the kitchen sink."[16]

In the title essay of *The White Album* Didion speaks of "a time when I began to doubt the premises of all the stories I had ever told myself. . . . I suppose this period began around 1966 and continued until 1971." She adds:

During those five years I appeared, on the face of it, a competent enough member of some community or another, a signer of contracts and Air Travel cards, a citizen. . . . It was a time of my life when I was frequently "named." I was named godmother to children. I was named lecturer and panelist, colloquist and conferee. I was even named, in 1968, a *Los Angeles Times* "Woman of the Year," along with Mrs. Ronald Reagan, the Olympic swimmer Debbie Meyer, and ten other California women who seemed to keep in touch and do good works. I did no good works but I tried to keep in touch. (pp. 11–12)

At approximately the same time as her public life was proceeding in such an orderly fashion, Didion was being treated for vertigo and nausea at the outpatient psychiatric clinic of St. John's Hospital in Santa Monica. There she was subjected to a number of tests, specifically to the Minnesota Multiphasic Personality Index, and the Rorshach, Thematic Appreciation, and Sentence Completion tests. Among other things, the ensuing psychiatric report describes *"a personality in process of deterioration with abundant signs of failing defenses and increasing inability of the ego to mediate the world of reality and to cope with normal stress"* (p. 14). This analysis was made in the summer of 1968 shortly after the author's attack of vertigo and nausea and shortly before she was named a *Los Angeles Times* Woman of the Year. "By way of comment," she writes, "I offer only that an attack of vertigo and nausea does not now seem to me an inappropriate response to the summer of 1968" (p. 15).

Shortly after the publication of *A Book of Common Prayer* Digby Diehl wrote a personality sketch of Didion entitled "Myth of Fragility Concealing a Tough Core." The reference here is, of course, to the fact that Didion's physical fragility masks her moral and intellectual toughness. (She has enjoyed success as a reporter, she tells us, because "I am so physically small, so temperamentally unobtrusive, and so neurotically inarticulate that people tend to forget that my presence runs counter to their best interests" [*Slouching*, p. xiv].) At five feet two and ninety-one pounds, Joan Didion does appear slight and delicate and she has been plagued by more than her share of ill health.[17] Accordingly, her writing is informed by an exquisite sensibility, forged at least in part by a feeling of personal vulnerability and by the experience of severe physical pain. She tells us, for example, that when she was writing the title essay of *Slouching Towards Bethlehem* she was "as sick as I have ever been": "The pain kept me awake at night and for twenty and twenty-one hours a day I drank gin and hot water to blunt the pain and took Dexedrine to blunt the gin and wrote the piece" (*Slouching*, p. xv). We get a glimpse into one of the main sources of her vulnerability and pain in the *White Album* essay "In Bed."

Didion, it seems, spends three, four, sometimes five days a month in bed with a migraine headache. And if she did not take drugs for her condition, she would be able to function only one day in four. She concedes that "the physiological error called migraine is . . . central to the given of my life" (p. 168). Yet there was a time when she was reluctant to make such an admission, when she thought it possible to rid herself of physiological error simply by denying its existence. "I fought migraine then," she writes, "ignored the warnings it sent, went to school and later to work in spite of it, sat through lectures in Middle English and presentations to advertisers with involuntary tears running down the right side of my face, threw up in washrooms, stumbled home by instinct, emptied ice trays onto my bed and tried to freeze the pain in my right temple, wished only for a neurosurgeon who would do a lobotomy on house call, and cursed my imagination" (p. 169).

After years of resistance, however, Didion finally got to the point where she accepted migraine as something with which she would have to live "the way some people live with diabetes." She no longer tries to fight it. Instead: "I lie down and let it happen. At first every small apprehension is magnified, every anxiety a pounding terror. Then the pain comes and I concentrate only on that." "Right there is the usefulness of migraine," she concludes; "there in that imposed yoga, the concentration on the pain. For when the pain recedes, ten or twelve hours later, everything goes with it, all the hidden resentments, all the vain anxieties. The migraine has acted as a circuit breaker, and the fuses have emerged intact. There is a pleasant convalescent euphoria. I open the windows and feel the air, eat gratefully, sleep well. I notice the particular nature of a flower in a glass on the stair landing. I count my blessings" (p. 172).

There is a certain type of individual who is particularly susceptible to migraine, "what doctors call a 'migraine personality.'" Such a personality "tends to be ambitious, inward, intolerant of error, rather rigidly organized, perfectionist." For Didion these characteristics "take the form of spending most of a week writing and rewriting and not writing a single paragraph" (p. 171). Also, they take the form of compulsive overreaching and of dissatisfaction with personal limitations. (At the age of eighteen, for example, the author wanted simultaneously to be a medieval scholar and a Rose Bowl princess.[18]) Moreover, one can perhaps see a migraine personality at work in Didion's continuing efforts to be—in addition to all else—a conventional mother and homemaker.

In "The Big Rock Candy Figgy Pudding Pitfall" (*Saturday Evening Post*, December 3, 1966) Didion writes: "I like to imagine myself a 'can-do' kind of woman, capable of patching the corral fence, pickling enough peaches to feed the hands all winter, and then winning a trip to Minneapolis in the Pillsbury Bake-Off. In fact, the day I stop believing that if put to it I could win the Pillsbury Bake-Off will signal the death of something."[19] What follows then is an amusing account of the author's plans one Christmas to make twenty hard-candy topiary trees and twenty figgy puddings (as in the carol lyric: "Oh bring us a figgy pudding and a happy new year"). We may conclude from the ensuing fiasco that Didion, far from being a "can-do" kind of woman, is suited only to doing what she is paid to do, "which is sit by myself and type with one finger." Here, she has typed a piece of domestic humor in the tradition of Jean Kerr and Erma Bombeck. If a film version of this sketch were to be made—a twenty-minute short, perhaps—the role of Didion would no doubt go to an actress with the comedic gifts of, say, Doris Day.

Miss Day, however, would probably not be capable of portraying the more complex protagonist of Didion's December 19, 1969, *Life* column, "In Praise of Unhung Wreaths and Love," for this essay is a painfully serious examination of the subject treated so engagingly in the earlier *Saturday Evening Post* sketch—the psychological and moral pressures of trying to fulfill a role for which one is temperamentally unsuited. The time is once again Christmas, but the scene is not California and home; instead, it is New York and "a bleak hotel room over a nightclub."[20]

Didion begins this essay by telling us of the idyllic sort of Christmas she had planned on having, of the house filled with candles and star jasmine, of the things that she and her daughter would do together. ("We would make pomegranate jelly and wrap the jars in red cellophane. We would sit at the piano and pick out carols together.") The fact that she is not home to do any of these things is, therefore, a source of guilt and self-doubt. "I suppose that it is some specter of failed love," she writes, "some chasm between the idea and the reality, that makes us wonder, come Christmas, if indeed we have been doing anything right. On the whole I do not think much about other people's expectations of me, but I do at Christmas."

She is in New York to write a movie about heroin users and she is typing her column "in a deserted office where the only suggestion of human life is the faint clatter of an untended AP wire." The next day she and Dunne are scheduled to interview a heroin dealer "in a Blimpy Burger on a desolate West Side street." Her contact promises to "be there around noon. . . . Or anyway between noon and four." As she contrasts her actual circumstances and surroundings with those of the idealized woman in her mind, that perfect homemaker hanging a wreath on her door in Los Angeles, she begins to cry. But she quickly gets hold of herself and refuses to indulge in facile self-reproach or self-pity. "Watching an AP wire in an empty office is precisely what I want to be doing," she says. "Women do not end up in empty offices and Blimpy Burgers by accident, any more than three-year-olds and their mothers need to make pomegranate jelly together to learn about family love." "The baby will know something about family love on Christmas," Didion concludes, "because she knows something about it today, and she will also know something about its complexities."

III *Woman of the Year*

In February 1969 the *Saturday Evening Post*—which claimed to have been founded by Ben Franklin in 1728—discontinued fortnightly publication (it would be revived on a quarterly basis in 1971) and, as a result, the "Points West" column also ceased to be. Later that year—December 1969—Didion began writing periodic features for *Life* and continued to do so through June 1970. In the next few years she also published in both the *New York Times Book Review* and the *New York Review of Books*. Then from February 1976 to December 1977 she and Dunne alternated writing a monthly column for *Esquire* called "The Coast." (A selection of her essays from this era of the 1970s and the late 1960s appeared in 1979 as *The White Album*.)

Moreover, during the 1970s Didion and Dunne worked on a number of motion picture screenplays—including *The Panic in Needle Park* (1971), the film version of *Play It as It Lays* (1972), and yet another remake of that Hollywood evergreen *A Star Is Born* (1976). (Although the idea for this remake was theirs, the Dunnes left the film prior to its completion. Speaking of the finished picture John Dunne says, "Put it this way, it's our beads, but it's not our necklace."[21]) And, perhaps most important, with the publication of *Play It as It Lays* in 1970 and *A Book of Common Prayer* in 1977 Joan Didion established herself as one of America's more talented contemporary novelists.

As a result of her critical and popular success Didion has become—if not a household word—at least a minor celebrity (she has been featured in *People* and *Self*[22] magazines and has been interviewed on NBC's "Tomorrow" show and on National Public Radio's "All Things Considered"). She discusses this newfound celebrity status in the *White Album* essay "On the Road." Here, she describes the promotional tour she made on behalf of *A Book of Common Prayer*—the press interviews she gave, the local talk shows on which she appeared, and that single question which she was constantly asked: "Where are we heading?" "The set for this discussion," Didion tells us, "was always the same: a cozy oasis of wicker and ferns in the wilderness of cables and cameras and Styrofoam coffee cups that was the actual studio. On wicker settees across the nation I expressed my conviction that we were heading 'into an era' of whatever the clock seemed to demand." (p. 175).

From this essay we derive a sense of the frenetic pace of life lived from airport to airport: "By the time I reached Boston," Didion writes, "ten days into the tour, I knew that I had never before heard and would possibly never again hear America singing at precisely this pitch: ethereal, speedy, an angel choir on Dexamyl" (p. 175). She "began to see America as my own, a child's map over which my child and I could skim and light at will. We spoke not of cities but of airports. If rain fell at Logan we could find sun at Dulles. Bags lost at O'Hare could be found at Dallas/Fort Worth" (p. 176).

If a large number of Didion's writings evoke memorable visual images, this one relies primarily on the author's ear for a particular kind of American speech. As she makes her rounds on the opinion circuit, certain trendy ideas and catch phrases get jumbled in surrealistic profusion. She "listened attentively . . . to people who seemed convinced that the 'texture' of their lives had been agreeably or adversely affected by conversion to the politics of joy, by regression to lapidary bleakness, by the Sixties, by the Fifties, by the recent change in administrations and by the sale of *The Thorn Birds* to paper for one-million-nine" (p. 178). And always there is that ubiquitous question: "Where are we heading?" "I don't know where you're heading," Didion says, "in the studio attached to the last of these antennae, my eyes fixed on still another of the neon FLEET-WOOD MAC signs that flickered that spring in radio stations from coast to coast, but I'm heading home" (p. 179). (It is, as a child might reckon it, a journey of threescore miles and ten. If your feet are nimble and light.)

CHAPTER 2

A Way of Saying I

WHEN examining Didion's views on literature one is struck by two diverse qualities. She is at once concerned with aesthetic beauty and with moral truth: while adept at numbering the streaks on the tulip, she is able to see beyond both the streaks and the tulip. Her most intensely personal observations tend not to be merely subjective; however, her epistemology is firmly rooted in the particular, the specific, and the concrete. In recalling her days at Berkeley she gives us an example of this latter characteristic. "I would try to contemplate the Hegelian dialectic," she writes, "and would find myself concentrating instead on a flowering pear tree outside my window and the particular way the petals fell on my floor. I would try to read linguistic theory and would find myself wondering instead if the lights were on in the bevatron up the hill."[1]

This revealing comment comes from the essay "Why I Write." In that essay Didion describes writing as "the act of saying *I*, of imposing oneself upon other people, of saying *listen to me, see it my way, change your mind*" (p. 2). Even the essay's title, which she admits to having "stolen" from George Orwell, is verbally suggestive. The vowel sound in all three words of the title, Didion points out, is that of the first person singular pronoun. It is, therefore, appropriate that she illustrate her theories about the creative process by recounting the circumstances which led to her own vocation as a writer.

It seems that Didion had trouble graduating from Berkeley because of her failure to take a course in Milton. "For reasons that now sound baroque," she writes, "I needed a degree by the end of that summer, and the English department finally agreed, if I would come down from Sacramento every Friday and talk about the cosmology of *Paradise Lost*, to certify me proficient in Milton" (p. 20). In complying with this plan she would sometimes take the Greyhound bus to Berkeley and at other times she would catch the Southern Pacific's City of San Francisco on the last leg of its transcontinental run. But today she admits:

I can no longer tell you whether Milton put the sun or the earth at the center of his universe in *Paradise Lost*, the central question of at least one century and a topic about which I wrote 10,000 words that summer, but I can still recall the exact rancidity of the butter in the City of San Francisco's dining car, and the way the tinted windows on the Greyhound bus cast the oil refineries around Carquinez Straits into a grayed and obscurely sinister light. In short my attention was always on the periphery, on what I could see and taste and touch, on the butter, and the Greyhound bus. (p. 2)

During those undergraduate years she came to realize that she was not meant to be a "scholar" or an "intellectual." "All I knew then," she writes, "was what I couldn't do. All I knew then was what I wasn't, and it took me some years to discover what I was.

"Which was a writer."

Perhaps it is an indication of how thoroughly romanticism has come to dominate our age that Didion would automatically assume a fundamental opposition between abstract speculation and concrete perception. (No doubt she would assent to William Carlos Williams's dictum, "No ideas but in things.") Accordingly, her very method of composition borders on the visionary: Faulkner heard voices; Didion sees "pictures that shimmer."[2] She tells us that although she is not schizophrenic and does not use hallucinogenic drugs, the shimmering pictures she sees are similar to the perceptions of those who do suffer from schizophrenia or who do ingest hallucinogenic drugs. Writing, for Didion, consists of finding the story which goes with a particular mental picture. And that "story" includes not just a sequence of events, but also the grammar which best articulates the meaning of those events. "The arrangement of the words matters, and the arrangement you want can be found in the picture in your mind. The picture dictates the arrangement" (p. 2).

An example of Didion's method of composition can be found in the creative evolution of her novel *A Book of Common Prayer*. She began with two pictures in her mind. One was of a newspaper photograph of a highjacked 707 burning in the Middle East. Another was of the night view from a hotel room on the Colombian coast in which she once spent a week with paratyphoid. But "the picture that shimmered and made these other images coalesce was the Panama airport at 6 A.M." (p. 98). Didion proceeds to describe the airport and to explain that she later made up a woman to put in the airport and a country to surround the airport and a family to rule said country. Finally, she found the proper narrative voice for her story by writing the following lines during her second week of work on the novel:

> I knew why Charlotte went to the airport even if
> Victor did not.
> I knew about airports.

When these lines were written Didion had no idea where Charlotte Douglas had been or why Charlotte went to airports. Nor did the author even have a character named Victor. "*I knew why Charlotte went to the airport*," she thought, "sounded incomplete. *I knew why Charlotte went to the airport even if Victor did not* carried a little more narrative drive" (p. 98). Thus, she was stuck with a character named Victor and with a narrator who knew both Charlotte and Victor. In order to acquaint herself with these characters and with the story in which they were involved it was necessary for Didion to write a novel. For her the act of creation is almost entirely a process of discovery.

In her comments on other writers Didion stresses the same qualities that are important in her own work. For example, she praises Graham Greene's eye for memorable detail and suggestive imagery, for what a character in one of his novels calls "marks of identity." She writes: "At his best, and his best is certainly *Brighton Rock*, Greene is a brilliant novelist precisely because he makes things so well, because he generates the kind of structural excitement that Flaubert gave to fiction, because he has an instinct for the novel that includes a certain sense of what people remember and how they dissemble and how they give themselves away."[3] Didion goes on to mention the fact that a character in Greene's *The End of the Affair* orders pork chops for lunch and that a character in *The Heart of the Matter* dislikes the borrowed rattan furniture in her home. "When Greene is good," Didion writes, he exhibits "the same sure feeling for fiction that Scott Fitzgerald sometimes exhibited (think of Tom and Daisy Buchanan eating that cold chicken in *Gatsby*, think of Pinkie and Rose on their wedding day in *Brighton Rock*)" (p. 191).

In addition to being a master stylist Greene is also a serious moralist. As such he is very much the sort of writer of whom Didion approves. While reviewing his novel *A Burnt-Out Case*, which she sees as being less than Greene's best, Didion makes some perceptive comments about the relation between religious belief and literary art. "Greene," she contends, "is not after all a 'great Catholic novelist' (a notion no less absurd that that of a 'great Low Episcopal novelist,' or of a 'great Trotskyist novelist')." Although "one can name dozens of novels indelibly informed by Christianity," novels which are primarily about redemption, "*Brighton Rock* and *The Heart of the Matter* are about human concern with redemption: another game entirely. Christianity is part of the *donnee* in a Greene novel; like heat on the west coast of Africa or V-1 raids in London, belief or the lack of it colors a decision, moves a scene, effects the dénouement, emerges as nothing more or less than one of the facts of the matter" (p. 190).

This particular review is one of approximately three dozen literary articles and notes which Didion published in *National Review* from 1959 to 1965. Some of the notes consist of only a short paragraph and several of the longer articles deal with works that are clearly minor; however, Didion also discusses major works by major writers. In going back over these essays and reviews and her other critical writings, we can begin to generalize about their author's literary sensibility. We can say, for example, that the writers whom she admires are—like Greene—expert craftsmen who also possess that quality which Matthew Arnold calls "high [moral] seriousness." For this reason, Didion refuses to excuse the moral lapses of even so fine a stylist as Salinger. (While conceding the technical virtues of *Franny and Zooey*, she takes its author to task for his "tendency to flatter the essential triviality within each of his readers."[4]) By the same token, she expresses her regard for such artists as Elizabeth Hardwick, Mary McCarthy, and Jean Stafford "because they are very good writers and because their writing reflects their respective moral sensibilities."[5] "I have a very rigid sense of right and wrong," she says. "What I mean is, I use the words all the time. Even the smallest things. A table can be right or wrong. . . . In order to maintain a semblance of purposeful behavior on this earth you have to believe that things are right or wrong."[6]

Just as she has little regard for amoral stylists, so too does Didion disapprove of artless polemicists. In her review of Doris Lessing's *Briefing for a Descent into Hell* (*Album*, pp. 119–25) she accuses Lessing of having written a novel entirely of ideas, "not a novel about the play of ideas in the lives of certain characters but a novel in which the characters exist only as markers in the presentation of an idea" (p. 120). Didion goes on to mention a slighting reference made by a character in another Lessing novel to writers who think in terms of artistic problems. Clearly, Didion rejects the dichotomy between life and art implicit in such a view. "*Madame Bovary* told us more about bourgeois life than several generations of Marxists have," she notes, "but there does not seem much doubt that Flaubert saw it as an artistic problem" (pp. 122–23). "That Mrs. Lessing does not," her critic concludes, "suggests her particular dilemma" (p. 123).

Ultimately, then, Didion does not equate moral art with mere didacticism. Although she does not consider technical brilliance to be the sole criterion for judging fiction, she nevertheless sees such brilliance as an essential characteristic of all good writing. One might even say that for Didion a novelist's primary—though not exclusive—*moral* obligation is to be a proficient craftsman.

While her literary opinions are to be found predominantly in her reviews of specific novels, Didion offers us a more general statement of her critical attitudes in her November 30, 1965, *National Review* essay, "Questions About the New Fiction." She begins this essay by noting the extent to which film has replaced fiction as the dominant topic at intellectual cocktail parties and other chic gatherings. She writes: "I wonder if . . . fascination with film is not symptomatic of a certain failure in fiction during the past several years, a failure to maintain the excitements of technical discipline, not only so apparent on, but so inflexibly imposed by film. It would be difficult in the extreme to 'improvise' a film successfully; the mechanics preclude it. Every setup makes a statement. . . . Skill at contrivance is the excitement of the exercise, and it is exactly the absence of this excitement which seems so marked in so many new novels" (p. 1100).

Those writers who come in for her overt or implied censure include Thomas Berger, Thomas Pynchon, J. P. Donleavy, Bruce Jay Friedman, Kurt Vonnegut, and Joseph Heller. She complains, for example, of Heller's "disinclination to go all the way with anything, his insistence on having it both ways, all ways, any way his fancy led." "For four hundred pages of *Catch-22*," she argues, "World War II was a fraud and the only virtue survival, while in the last few pages we learned that the war was worth fighting but some of the officers were maniacs, a rather different proposition" (p. 1101).

Finally, Didion tries to point the way in which literature should be moving and to indicate which writers already are headed in that direction: "Everyone wants to tell the truth, and everyone recognizes that to juxtapose even two sentences is necessarily to tell a lie, to tell less than one knows, to distort the situation, cut off its ambiguities and so its possibilities. To write with style is to fight lying all the way. Nonetheless, this is what must be done or we end up maundering. We tell nothing. To tell something, really tell it, takes a certain kind of moral hardness" (p. 1101). Her list of those who possess this moral hardness includes: Norman Mailer, John Hawkes, Bernard Malamud, Flannery O'Connor, Vladimir Nabokov (sometimes), John Cheever, Katherine Anne Porter, and Saul Bellow (in *Seize the Day* but not in *Herzog*).

Of course, by following her principles, one could expand Didion's lists—both of praise and of censure. The salient point, however, is that, by telling us what she values in literature, she is also suggesting standards by which she wants her own work to be judged. According to those standards Joan Didion belongs in the ranks of those who tenaciously fight the lie, of those who, in her own words, "display what was once called character" (*Slouching*, p. 145).[7]

CHAPTER 3

The Center Cannot Hold

IN her review of John Cheever's *Falconer* Joan Didion writes:

> Some of us are not Jews. Neither are some of us Southerners, nor children of the Iroquois, nor the inheritors of any other notably dark and bloodied ground. Some of us are even Episcopalians. In the popular mind this absence of any particular claim on the conscience of the world is generally construed as a historical advantage, but in the small society of those who read and write it renders us "different," and a little suspect. . . . Yet in a very real way the white middle-class Protestant writer in America is in fact homeless—as absent from the world of his fathers as he is "different" within the world of letters.[1]

Didion's use of the first-person plural here is no mere rhetorical gesture. Just as her writings about California (see Chapter 7) reflect a note of homelessness similar to the one she finds so pervasive in Cheever's fiction, so too does her critical and moral sensibility render her "different within the world of letters." (Indeed, her definition of that sensibility in terms of a white middle-class Protestant ethos reminds one vaguely of Eliot's claim to be "classicist in literature, royalist in politics, and anglo-catholic in religion.") In her observations about politics, morality, and the general malaise of our culture she articulates a position of personal integrity which runs counter to the prevailing norms of relativism. Her ethnic, social, and religious heritage gives her a sense of historical identity, without imposing parochial restraints upon her judgment and imagination. She is an unsentimental humanist who happens to be of a particular time, to have come from a particular place.

I *A Majority of One*

On a number of occasions Didion has commented on her aversion to politics.[2] For example, she says to Sara Davidson, "I never had faith that the answers to human problems lay in anything that could be called political. I thought the answers, if there were answers, lay someplace in man's soul" ("Visit," p. 36). One should not conclude, however, that Didion is indifferent to public issues, only that her political opinions run counter to conventional ideology. Such ideology, on both the right and the left, consists of strange mixtures of authoritarianism and anarchism. For the most part the right advocates strong government action in the areas of domestic law enforcement and national defense, but supports only limited government interference in the marketplace. In contrast, the left sees the proper function of government in approximately opposite terms. Joan Didion, however, would probably concur with Thoreau that "that government is best which governs not at all."

She tells Davidson, "The ethic I was raised in was specifically a Western frontier ethic. That means being left alone and leaving others alone. . . . The politics I personally want are anarchic. Throw out the laws. Tear it down. Start all over. That is very romantic because it presumes that, left to their own devices, people would do good things for one another. I doubt that that's true. But I would like to believe it" (p. 36). In point of fact, Didion's view of human nature is anything but sanguine. She seems to believe, however, that our *individual* foibles and cruelties are to be preferred to the systematized evils of group action. According to such a view, the surest way to make things worse is to organize for the purpose of making them better. Because of the evenhandedness of her anarchism Didion alternately criticizes political movements of every ideological stripe. She is a partisan not of "causes" but of the individual human spirit.

In "Comrade Laski CPUSA (M-L)" (*Slouching*, pp. 61-66) and the *Saturday Evening Post* columns "Black Panther" (May 4, 1968) and "The Revolution Game" (January 25, 1969) Didion discusses, in tones of quiet irony, various permutations of radical politics in America. The first of these essays deals with Michael Laski, a twenty-six-year-old UCLA dropout who is general secretary of a revolutionary Maoist cadre. Like so many fringe sects of the left, Laski's group—the Communist party USA (Marxist-Leninist)—seems less concerned with restructuring society than with questioning the ideological soundness of other true believers. The group "is rigidly committed to . . . the notions that the traditional American Communist Party is a 'revisionist bourgeois clique,' that the Progressive Labor Party, the Trotskyites, and 'the revisionist clique headed by Gus Hall' prove themselves opportunistic bourgeois lackeys by making their peace appeal not to the 'workers' but to the liberal imperialists; and that H. Rap Brown is the tool, if not the conscious agent, of the ruling imperialist class" (pp. 61-62).

Didion views Laski's situation more in psychological and meta-physical than in doctrinal terms. She tells us that she is "comfortable with the Michael Laskis of this world, with those who live outside rather than in, those in whom the sense of dread is so acute that they turn to extreme and doomed commitments." "I know something about dread myself," she continues, "and appreciate the elaborate systems with which some people manage to fill the void, appreciate all the opiates of the people, whether they are as accessible as alcohol and heroin and promiscuity or as hard to come by as faith in God or History" (pp. 62–63). She completes her essay with a description of one of the party's diurnal rituals—Comrade Simmons's report on the day's receipts from sale of the revolutionary tabloid *People's Voice*. When queried about the paucity of his take Simmons replies, "It's always bad the day before welfare and unemployment checks arrive" (p. 66). "You see what the world of Michael Laski is," Didion concludes, "a minor but perilous triumph of being over nothingness" (p. 66).

If Michael Laski is an obscure ideologue, Black Panther founder Huey P. Newton is a celebrity dissident. Shortly after his arrest on charges of murdering a white policeman, Newton became the focus of large-scale protest rallies in the San Francisco Bay area. Joan Didion describes the ambience of one such rally as follows:

LET'S SPRING HUEY, the buttons said (50 cents each), and here and there on the courthouse steps, among the Black Panthers with their berets and sunglasses, the chants would go up:
> Get your M-31,
> 'Cause baby we gonna have some fun,
> BOOM, BOOM, BOOM, BOOM.
"Fight on, brother," a woman would add in the spirit of a good-natured amen. "Bang, bang." There were always whites there as well, some of them the cause-proud who had spent all their adult lives shoring up their virtue by passing out leaflets on rainy mornings around Oakland and Berkeley and San Francisco. . . .
James Forman came, and told the Panthers and their black and white admirers that whereas the retaliation they were to extract in the case of his own death should only be 10 war factories, 15 power plants, 30 police stations, one southern governor, two mayors and 50 cops, "for Huey Newton the sky's the limit." Rap Brown came. "The only thing that's gonna free Huey Newton," he told them, "is gunpowder." Stokely Carmichael came, and he told them this: "Huey Newton laid down his life for us."[3]

Didion points out, quite rightly, that Huey had not yet laid down his life for anyone. Nevertheless, Carmichael's statement suggests the political utility of Newton's position. "In many ways," Didion writes, "he was more useful to the revolution behind bars than on the street. It was the fact of his being behind bars, after all, that attracted attention, that enabled Huey Newton to give . . . press conferences." The supreme head of the Black Panthers may ultimately be a victim of self-delusion; he may not fully understand the irony of what he has become. "In the politics of revolution everyone is expendable, but . . . the value of a Scottsboro boy is easier to see if you are not yourself the Scottsboro boy."

In contrast to the lethal seriousness of Huey Newton's dilemma, the atmosphere surrounding political protests at San Francisco State was positively festive. Didion, in her final *Saturday Evening Post* column, describes the campus turmoil which, among other things, launched S. I. Hayakawa into national prominence. Seeming to disdain both left and right, she refuses to take the protests seriously— either as idealistic struggle or as threat to the body politic.

She recalls a note which was scrawled on the door of the campus cafeteria one morning: "Adjetprop committee meeting in the Redwood Room."

Only someone who needed very badly to be alarmed could respond with force to a guerrilla band that not only announced its meetings on the enemy's bulletin board but seemed innocent of the spelling, and so the meaning, of the words it used. "Hitler Hayakawa," some of the faculty began calling S. I. Hayakawa, the semanticist who became the college's third president in a year and incurred considerable displeasure by trying to keep the campus open. "*Eichmann*," Kay Boyle screamed at him at a rally. Subtlety of invective was not in high supply at San Francisco State.[4]

Despite the inflammatory nature of such rhetoric, the strike "simply never seemed serious. . . . The climate inside the Administration Building was that of a college musical. Striking black militants dropped in to chat with the deans; striking white radicals exchanged gossip in the corridors. 'No chance we'll be open tomorrow,' secretaries informed callers. 'Go skiing, have a good time.' The scene seemed to lack only Peter Lawford and June Allyson."

Didion is probably correct in suggesting that the "crisis" at San Francisco State is the stuff of which Evelyn Waugh novels are made; and, like Waugh, she possesses a finely developed sense of the absurd. She describes, for example, a meeting of the campus SDS: "They listened to a student who had driven up for the day from the College of San Mateo, a junior college down the peninsula from San Francisco [and located in one of the wealthiest counties in Califor-

nia]. 'I came up here today with some Third World students to
tell you that we're with you, and we hope you'll be with *us* when we try
to pull off a strike next week, because we're really into it, we carry our
motorcycle helmets all the time, can't think, can't go to class. . . . I'm
here to tell you that at College of San Mateo we're living like
revolutionaries.'"

It probably would not have been possible for a woman as
prominent as Joan Didion—writing in the United States during the
late 1960s and early 1970s—to avoid defining her position in regard
to women's liberation. Accordingly, her original and suggestive essay
"The Women's Movement" (*Album*, pp. 109–18) does examine the
flowering of American feminism and, in the process, manages to
avoid the pitfalls of cant and jargon. Its underlying thesis seems to be
that the revolutionary rhetoric of the women's movement belies that
movement's actual appeal to limited goals of self-fulfillment. In this
regard, at least, feminism is no different from any other radical cause
in American history.

Traditionally, Didion argues, the have-nots of our society have
"aspired mainly to having. . . . They resisted that essential inductive
leap from the immediate reform to the social ideal, and, just as
disappointingly, they failed to perceive their common cause with
other minorities, continued to exhibit a self-interest disconcerting in
the extreme to organizers steeped in the rhetoric of 'brotherhood'"
(p. 110). As a result, the upward mobility of those who were formerly
disadvantaged threatened to foreclose the possibility of massive
social revolution.

And then, at that exact dispirited moment when there seemed no one at all
willing to play the proletariat, along came the women's movement, and the
invention of women as a "class." One could not help admiring the radical
simplicity of this instant transfiguration. The notion that, in the absence of a
cooperative proletariat, a revolutionary class might simply be invented,
made up, "named" and so brought into existence, seemed at once so
pragmatic and so visionary, so precisely Emersonian, that it took the breath
away, exactly confirmed one's idea of where nineteenth-century transcenden-
tal instincts, crossed with a late reading of Engels and Marx, might lead. (pp.
110–11)

The reason Didion finds herself at odds with feminist ideology is
that—like all ideologies—feminism tends to blunt those moral
distinctions and ambiguities which most interest her. "To believe in
'the greater good,'" she writes, "is to operate, necessarily, in a certain

ethical suspension. Ask anyone committed to Marxist analysis how many angels on the head of a pin, and you will be asked in return to never mind the angels, tell me who controls the production of pins" (p. 112).

The author also argues that—contrary to popular misconceptions—not all feminists are hard and resourceful. Some, she tells us, even write of "the intolerable humiliations of being observed by construction workers on Sixth Avenue." Indeed, such a grievance "seemed always to take on unexplored Ms. Scarlett overtones, suggestions of fragile, cultivated flowers being 'spoken to,' and therefore violated, by uppity proles" (p. 113). Much the same argument is advanced in her commentary on lesbian literature: she is struck by its "emphasis on the superior 'tenderness' of the relationship, the 'gentleness' of the sexual connection, as if the participants were wounded birds." "The derogation of assertiveness as 'machismo'" she contends, "has achieved such currency that one imagines several million women too delicate to deal at any level with an overtly heterosexual man" (p. 116).

"It was a long way," Didion concludes, "from Simone de Beauvoir's grave and awesome recognition of woman's role as 'the Other' to the notion that the first step in changing that role was Alix Kates Shulman's marriage contract ("wife strips beds, husband remakes them"), a document reproduced in *Ms.,* but it was toward just such trivialization that the women's movement seemed to be heading" (p. 113). And as if to confirm this trend, a writer for *Ms.* recently confessed to finding Didion's argument "almost impossible to understand."[5]

Intellectual obtuseness and self-delusion are, of course, not exclusively qualities of the women's movement, for these traits can be found everywhere. The pretensions of political activists, however, seem to constitute a particularly apt target for ridicule; if only because said pretensions are usually grander in design than those of ordinary people. Consider, for example, the behavior of certain upper-class liberals. Such individuals, according to their detractors, are moral elitists who, through a sense of guilt or a desire for romance, are led to identify themselves with the plight of the dispossessed. (A Mother Teresa or an Albert Schweitzer can achieve virtual sainthood through a life of genuine sacrifice, but most of the rest of us are willing to pay only perfunctory obeisance before the ikon of human brotherhood.)

The elitist liberal's capacity for self-parody may not be boundless, but it is extensive enough to inspire polemicists like William Buckley

and social critics like Tom Wolfe. Indeed, Wolfe's 1970 essays
Radical Chic and *Mau-Mauing the Flak Catchers* have become
minor classics of antiestablishment satire. Some of Joan Didion's
journalism of the 1960s, however, anticipates both the tone and thesis
of Wolfe's more extensive and more famous reportage. In this regard
one thinks particularly of her discussion of a visionary west-coast
"think tank" in "California Dreaming" (*Slouching*, pp. 73–78) and of
Hollywood political involvement in "Good Citizens" (*Album*,
pp. 86–89).

The first of these essays focuses on Santa Barbara's Center for the
Study of Democratic Institutions. A sort of floating seminar, the
center "is supported on the same principle as a vanity press. People
who are in a position to contribute large sums of money are
encouraged to participate in clarifying the basic issues" of the day
(p. 77). The driving force behind this project is former University of
Chicago president Dr. Robert M. Hutchins, an educator who once
tried to catalogue "The 102 Great Ideas of Western Man." At his
think tank Hutchins fosters a kind of reverse intellectual snobbism.
"The place is in fact avidly anti-intellectual," Didion tells us, "the
deprecatory use of words like 'egghead' and 'ivory tower' reaching
heights matched only in a country-club locker room. Hutchins takes
pains to explain that by 'an intellectual community' he does not mean
a community 'whose members regard themselves as "intellectuals"'"
(p. 76).

On a given day at the center one might encounter founding member
Dinah Shore discussing civil rights with Bayard Rustin or hear
founding member Kirk Douglas speak "his piece on 'The Arts in a
Democratic Society'" (p. 77). Then there is "concerned citizen" Jack
Lemmon. "'Apropos of absolutely nothing,' Mr. Lemmon says,
pulling on a pipe, 'just for my own amazement—I don't *know*, but I
want to know—.' At this juncture he wants to know about student
unrest, and, at another, he worries that government contracts will
corrupt 'pure research.'" Concerned citizen Paul Newman muses:
"'You mean maybe they get a grant to develop some new kind of
plastic,' . . . and Mr. Lemmon picks up the cue: 'What happens then
to the humanities?'" (p. 78).

For a much fuller description of politically concerned celebrities
we need only turn to Didion's discussion of liberal Hollywood, a
community whose public life "comprises a kind of dictatorship of
good intentions, a social contract in which actual and irreconcilable
disagreement is as taboo as failure or bad teeth, a climate devoid of
irony" (*Album*, pp. 86–87). It is also a climate in which one can hear

once or twice a week "that no man is an island . . . , quite often from people who think they are quoting Ernest Hemingway" (p. 86).

The specific occasion for Didion's essay is her visit to a Beverly Hills nightclub called Eugene's. The club is run by supporters of Senator Eugene McCarthy on behalf of McCarthy's 1968 campaign for the Democratic presidential nomination. Not unlike that campaign itself, Eugene's "had a certain *deja vu* aspect to it, a glow of 1952 humanism: there were Ben Shahn posters on the walls, and the gesture toward a strobe light was nothing that might interfere with 'good talk,' and the music was not 1968 rock but the kind of jazz people used to have on their record players when everyone who believed in the Family of Man bought Scandinavian stainless-steel flatware and voted for Adlai Stevenson" (p. 87). It was "there at Eugene's" that Didion "heard the name 'Erich Fromm' for the first time in a long time, and many other names cast out for the sympathetic magic they might work" (p. 87).[6]

Didion is willing to concede that the main event of that evening at Eugene's—a debate between Ossie Davis and William Styron on the probable effect of Styron's *The Confessions of Nat Turner* on race relations in America—certainly did "no harm and perhaps some good." And yet, she continues, "its curious vanity and irrelevance stay with me, if only because those qualities characterize so many of Hollywood's best intentions" (p. 88). "Social problems," she concludes, "present themselves to many of these people in terms of a scenario. . . . Marlon Brando does not, in a well-plotted motion picture, picket San Quentin in vain: what we are talking about here is faith in a dramatic convention. Things 'happen' in motion pictures. There is always a resolution, always a strong cause-effect dramatic line, and to perceive the world in those terms is to assume an ending for every social scenario" (p. 88).

Although conservatives also deal in social scenarios many of which are just as vain and irrelevant as those of their brethren on the left, Didion has yet to focus her satirical scrutiny on the organized political right. One can find in her journalism, however, a skeptical attitude toward many of the beliefs cherished by that group of Americans which Richard Nixon dubbed "the great silent majority." A case in point is her February 20, 1970, *Life* column, "On the Last Frontier with VX and GB." In this article she writes of the federal government's intention to store a vast shipment of VX and GB nerve gas on 20,000 acres outside Hermiston, Oregon. The gas would be contained in regular mounds of "reinforced concrete covered with sod and sagebrush, 1,001 mounds rising from the earth in staggered rows and laced with fifty miles of rail track."[7] In a beautifully understated style Didion concentrates less on the government's plans than on the response in Hermiston toward those plans.

Still flush with the boom spirit of the frontier, the townspeople are certain that by storing the nerve gas in their community, and thus boosting the town's economy, they will also be performing a patriotic service. "I was in Hermiston for a couple of days," Didion writes, "before I began to realize where I was . . . that I was not in a frontier town at all but in a post-frontier town, which was always a little different."

What was happening now in . . . [Hermiston] was precisely what happened all over the West, after the neurasthenics and the mystics had moved on and the settlers moved in. I was in a place where people felt, just as other settlers had felt in the waning days of other frontiers, somehow redeemed, cut free from the ambiguities of history. They could afford their innocent blend of self-interest and optimism. They still had a big country and a big sky and cheap expendable land, and they could still tap the Columbia for all the water and power they needed and the best was still to come, or so they thought.

The people of Hermiston, as Didion depicts them, seem like updated figures from a Sinclair Lewis novel (especially the old-timers in *Main Street*'s postfrontier Gopher Prairie). We read, for example, of Joe Burns, "a mild-mannered funeral director who had helped draft a letter to President Nixon saying how much the citizens of Hermiston wanted the extra nerve gas." When queried about the possible safety hazards posed by the gas, Burns replies: "They talk about a few drops of it killing thousands of people. Well, really, you'd need pretty ideal conditions for that. And if you give yourself an injection within 30 seconds, there's no effect whatsoever." Apparently his position is fairly representative of that of his fellow townspeople. The good folks of Hermiston believe that those who oppose the nerve gas are "from Portland and Eugene and somehow under the sway of . . . 'the academic-community-Moratorium-and-other-mothers-for-peace-or-whatever.'"

Didion's condescension toward the jejune optimism of these people is neither cruel nor strident. Instead, it is like the indulgent and wistful condescension that an adult might show toward a child's innocence. (In *Bright Book of Life*, Alfred Kazin discusses Didion's work in a chapter on women writers entitled "Cassandras." And it is precisely through the persona of an unheeded prophetess that Didion maintains her ironic perspective on these expansive Oregonians.) She concludes: "They believed in 'growth,' in 'the future,' in 'doubling the population' as an unequivocal good. Where I come from in California, we have already seen the future and it does not work, but there was no way of telling anyone that on the last frontier."

In "Fathers, Sons, and Screaming Eagles" (*Saturday Evening Post*, October 19, 1968) Didion examines another group of solid American citizens. Her topic here is the generation gap as viewed from the perspective of the 101st Airbourne Association's twenty-third annual reunion "one weekend in Las Vegas not long ago."[8] As one might expect, her descriptions of Las Vegas and of the reunited veterans ("screaming eagles" as they call themselves) are brilliantly precise and economical: "There were telegrams to be sent, to the 101st in Vietnam ('Keep that Eagle Screaming'), and telegrams to be read, from Hubert Humphrey ('We are not a nation that has lost its way, but a nation seeking a better way'). There was even a Teen Room where a handful of children sat on folding chairs and regarded a Wurlitzer with sullen ennui."

The substance of this essay, however, concerns the difference between Vietnam and World War II. This difference is clearly suggested by the contrast between what some of the veterans think about their own experiences and how they view the war which their sons are being called upon to fight. (The men at the reunion had had "a great adventure, an essential adventure, and almost every-one . . . had been 19 and 20 years old when they had it, and they had survived and come home and their wives had given birth to sons, and now those sons were 19, 20, and perhaps it was not such a great adventure this time.")

During her stay in Las Vegas Didion encounters a veteran named Skip Skivington, a man in his early forties whose son is missing in Vietnam. At the beginning of the essay we see Skivington showing the author a newspaper story and a snapshot of his son, preserved in clear plastic. "I gave the clipping back to Skip Skivington," she says, "and before he put it back in his pocket again he looked at it a long while, smoothed out an imagined crease and studied the fragment of newsprint as if it held some answer."

Didion structures her essay symmetrically, closing with a second screaming eagle—Walter Davis—talking about his son. Davis had jumped into Holland in 1944, now works for the Metropolitan Life in Lawndale, California, and has three children, including a son of 14. He describes with relish the excitement and romance of his service in Europe. But when Didion mentions the plight of Skip Skivington's son, Davis admits that during his own youth he had never contemplated the hazards of war. Now, however, he has a son who will reach draft age in four years. "Walter Davis broke open a roll, buttered it carefully, and put it down again untouched. 'I see it a little differently now,' he said."

Although we never learn the fate of Walter Davis's son, or of Skip Skivington's, one of Didion's 1970 *Life* columns—"Ten Long Minutes in Punchbowl"—does describe the burial of an *unnamed* casualty of Vietnam. This sketch—which remains substantially intact as part of a *White Album* sequence entitled "In the Islands"—is not an antiwar polemic; however, in the austere objectivity of her prose Didion makes a powerfully effective statement about the human costs of armed conflict.[9]

Her setting is Punchbowl, more formally known as the National Memorial Cemetery of the Pacific, a military graveyard located in an extinct volcano near Honolulu. There are 19,500 graves in Punchbowl, 13,000 of which are a result of World War II. Some of the remaining dead were killed in Korea and a fraction of the total come from Vietnam. Of the latter most are island boys, but a few are brought back across the Pacific by their families from the mainland.

Didion visits Punchbowl and speaks with its superintendent, Mr. Corley. "We were sitting in his office in the crater and on the wall hung the Bronze Star and Silver Star citations he had received in Europe in 1944, Martin T. Corley, a man in an aloha shirt who had somehow gone from South Ozone Park in Queens to the Battle of the Bulge to a course in cemetery management at Fort Sam Houston and finally, twenty-some years later, to an office in an extinct volcano in the Pacific from which he could watch the quick and the dead in still another war" (*Album*, p. 141). That day Didion is invited to witness the burial of a California boy killed in Vietnam. "Two of us from the office come to all the Vietnams," Mr. Corley explains, "I mean in case the family breaks down or something" (p. 142).

Recalling the funeral, the author says,

All I can tell you about the next ten minutes is that they seemed a very long time. We watched the coffin being carried to the grave and we watched the pallbearers lift the flag, trying to hold it taut in the warm trade wind. The wind was blowing hard, toppling the vases of gladioli set by the grave, obliterating some of the chaplain's words. . . . I was looking beyond the chaplain to a scattering of graves so fresh they had no headstones, just plastic markers stuck in the ground. "We tenderly commit this body to the ground," the chaplain said then. The men in the honor guard raised their rifles. Three shots cracked out. The bugler played taps. The pallbearers folded the flag

until only the blue field and a few stars showed, and one of them stepped
forward to present the flag to the father. (pp. 142–43)

As the mourners begin to depart, "the father, transferring the flag
from hand to hand as if it burned, said a few halting words to the
pallbearers." Mr. Corley is careful to see that the grave is quickly
covered because he does not like for families to return to the
mainland worrying about whether the burial has been completed.
"We cover them within thirty minutes," he says. "Fill, cover, get the
marker on. That's one thing I remember from my training" (pp.
143–44).

The ritual completed, Didion leaves Punchbowl, her final perceptions burned in the memory like figures etched with acid. "We
stood there a moment in the warm wind," she writes, "then said goodbye. The pallbearers filed onto the Air Force bus. The bugler walked
past, whistling 'Raindrops Keep Fallin' on My Head.' Just after four
o'clock the father and mother came back and looked for a long while
at the covered grave, then took a night flight back to the mainland.
Their son was one of 101 Americans killed that week in Vietnam"
(p. 144).

II *The Moral Imagination*

Despite her claim of not being an intellectual, Didion does address
herself on occasion to abstract ethical and philosophical issues. She
does so, for example, in her essay "On Morality," which originally
appeared in the *American Scholar*, and in four other moral essays, all
originally in *Vogue*. Although she illustrates her arguments here with
concrete and personal references, her concern in each of these essays
is with *fundamental* questions of human nature. Characteristically,
her approach to these questions is that of a sensitive, but tough-
minded, individualist.

Not unlike her political outlook, Joan Didion's moral philosophy
is heavily tinged with epistemological skepticism. She believes very
strongly in the objective reality of good and evil, but she does not
think herself capable of deciding what is right and wrong for all
persons in all cases. Thus she holds very tenaciously to those few
moral precepts of which she is certain, while generally distrusting
reform movements and what she calls "The Insidious Ethic of
Conscience."[10] In "On Morality" Didion writes: "Except on the most
primitive level—our loyalties to those we love—what could be more
arrogant than to claim the primacy of personal conscience? ('Tell me,'

a rabbi asked Daniel Bell when he said, as a child, that he did not believe in God. 'Do you think God cares?')" (*Slouching*, p. 161).

As one might expect, the sort of morality which Didion does endorse is an elemental frontier ethic. It is a "social code that is sometimes called . . . 'wagon-train morality'" (p. 158). To illustrate this social code she tells us about an automobile accident which took place in Death Valley. One night a car hit the shoulder of the road and the young man who was driving was killed instantly. His female companion, though still alive, was bleeding internally, deep in shock. A nurse drove the girl to the nearest doctor, "185 miles across the floor of the Valley and three ranges of lethal mountain road" (p. 157), while the nurse's husband stayed with the boy's body. Didion explains that "if a body is left alone for even a few minutes on the desert, the coyotes close in and eat the flesh." "Whether or not a corpse is torn apart by coyotes," she continues, "may seem only a sentimental consideration, but of course it is more: one of the promises we make to one another is that we will try to retrieve our casualties, try not to abandon our dead to the coyotes. If we have been taught to keep our promises—if, in the simplest terms, our upbringing is good enough—we stay with the body, or have bad dreams" (p. 158).[11]

"On Self-Respect" (*Slouching*, pp. 142–48) and the unanthologized *Vogue* columns "Take No for an Answer" (October 1, 1961), "Emotional Blackmail: An Affair of Every Heart" (November 15, 1962), and "Jealousy: Is It a Curable Illness" (June 1961) all deal with the question of moral and emotional integrity. One need only compare these judicious and literate essays with the more superficial self-help books of recent years to realize the extent to which Didion's work transcends the fashions of popular culture. In the first of these essays she begins by speaking of a kind of immature self-regard which most of us lose as we grow older. For Joan Didion such a loss came when she failed to be elected to Phi Beta Kappa. This setback "marked the end of something, and innocence may well be the word for it" (p. 142). "I faced myself that day," she confides, "with the nonplussed apprehension of someone who has come across a vampire and has no crucifix at hand" (p. 143).

Genuine self-respect, however, is a more mature and durable quality. It is a quality "that our grandparents, whether or not they had it, knew all about. They had instilled in them, young, a certain discipline, the sense that one lives by doing things one does not particularly want to do, by putting fears and doubts to one side, by weighing immediate comforts against the possibility of larger, even intangible comforts."

It seemed to the nineteenth century admirable, but not remarkable, that Chinese Gordon put on a clean white suit and held Khartoum against the Mahdi. . . . To say that Waterloo was won on the playing fields of Eton is not to say that Napoleon might have been saved by a crash program in cricket; to give formal dinners in the rain forest would be pointless did not the candlelight flickering on the liana call forth deeper, stronger disciplines, values instilled long before. It is a kind of ritual, helping us to remember who and what we are. In order to remember it, one must have known it. (pp. 145–46, 147)

One of the consequences of insufficient self-respect is explored in "Take No for an Answer." Indeed, this essay is actually about the inability of some people to give "no" for an answer. Such people, Didion argues, are generally so insecure in their self-image that they will go to elaborate lengths in order to avoid displeasing others. "Forced to please everyone," she writes, "we usually end up pleasing no one—least of all those we should want most to please. It is easier to snarl at one's husband than to tell a casual acquaintance that one is too busy to see him; easier to disappoint one's father than to refuse a favour to someone one scarcely knows. One's father and husband, after all, can be won again; the rest of the world must be won now or not at all" (p. 133).

To lose the ability to say "no"—assuming that one had it in the first place—is to live in a state of multiple schizophrenia and confusion. Didion describes such a state in terms of an archetypal dream "—a nightmare, really—in which one is pushed onto a stage just as the curtain rises. Because it is too late to find out what the play is, let alone what part one is expected to play, one can only watch nervously for clues" (p. 133). The dreamer has, quite simply, experienced a loss of identity. He has come to exist so totally "in the approval of others" that he has finally lost all sense of his "own wants and needs" (p. 133). "Something seems to have been mislaid, and it is futile to look in the drawer with the birth certificate, the passport, and the *Book of Common Prayer* inscribed by the Bishop; useless to call the lost-and-found, pointless to wonder whether one had it that day on the New Haven. The article lost would be hard to describe. *When did I last have myself?*" (p. 133).

Those who do not have themselves frequently pay emotional blackmail in order to purchase a false image of themselves. In describing just such a phenomenon Didion recalls an acquaintance of hers who was bold enough and unscrupulous enough to make excessive demands on people, confident that they would comply. "Some of us loved him and some of us did not," she remembers, "but whether we did or not we all acquiesced, helpless before the undertone his every plea carried: I need you. . . . We would see in his reproachful eyes, suddenly, the sister we had failed, the friend we had hurt—all the opportunities for goodness or glory or marks in heaven we had ever muffed, miserably. In brief, he could expose us to ourselves, and we quite flatly bought him off" (p. 117).

But emotional blackmail, like its more conventional counterpart, is never paid in full. "As Rudyard Kipling once wrote, 'If once you have paid him the Danegeld/You are never rid of the Dane'" (p. 117). To rid oneself of both the Danegeld and the Dane is finally to discard false images of the self, to live with all the vices and shortcomings that will forever preclude one's canonization. It is "a feat of such epic proportions that those attempting it sometimes seem in the grip of advanced autonarcosis" (p. 117).

Finally, we turn to Didion's discussion of jealousy—a condition intimately bound up with one's sense of self. "Descartes once described the emotion as a 'life-conserving tendency,' Dr. Arnold Gesell as 'synonymous almost with the will to live.' A noun derived, not entirely incidentally, from the Greek *zelos*, or zeal, jealousy is born of the instinct toward preservation of self: one can be jealous only of something or someone perceived as an extension of oneself" (p. 96). (The ultimate egalitarian, jealousy resides among the blessed as well as among the damned. "Although one finds it difficult to imagine Cleopatra afflicted with jealousy (the notion is ludicrous, rather like imagining her laid up with migraine on that perfumed barge, equipped with Fiorinal and an ice bag), she wanted to know the height of Antony's bride, to know the colour of her hair" [p. 96].)

While jealousy is not an inherently bad thing (indeed, some people find it to be a therapeutic escape from other, more intractable problems), a person who allows it to reach pathological extremes can become emotionally crippled. (Such a person is usually dissatisfied with himself; he dreams of being someone else—anyone else.) Such a person, however, is in the minority. For most of us "jealousy is neither crippler nor escape. It is instead the rare but piercing chill in the night, the waste of emotion better spent on loving. Better spent, for that matter, on cleaning closets" (p. 97).

Didion concludes that the cure for pathological jealousy involves a degree of self-knowledge and self-acceptance. "What debilitates and finally destroys is the beast that stays in the jungle. . . . To accept the fact that jealousy begins with self-discontent is to change the locus of the threat from outside to within, to take the first step . . . toward becoming what Criseyde claimed to be but never was: *myn owene womman, wel at ese*" (p. 97).

III *Vexed To Nightmare*

"Many people I know in Los Angeles believe that the Sixties ended abruptly on August 9, 1969, ended at the exact moment when word of the murders on Cielo Drive traveled like brushfire through the community, and in a sense this is true. The tension broke that day. The paranoia was fulfilled" (*Album*, p. 47). The murders being referred to are those of Sharon Tate Polanski, Abigail Folger, Jay Sebring, Voytek Frykowski, Steven Parent, and Rosemary and Leno LaBianca; and the passage itself is fairly typical of the title essay of *The White Album*.[12] This essay consists of fifteen loosely connected scenes from the late 1960s, scenes which include matters of public concern—such as the Huey Newton case and the rebellion at San Francisco State—and moments of private crisis in the author's own life. Didion is attempting, through the mood of physical and psychic violence which pervades these fifteen scenes, to convey a sense of American experience at a particular historical moment.

We learn, for example, that the author avidly studied the trial of the Ferguson brothers—killers of silent screen star Ramon Novarro—and that she came to know Manson follower Linda Kasabian rather well. For Didion these names obviously have a kind of totemic significance. (Since things other than brutal murders occurred during the late 1960s,[13] the author's choice of emphasis suggests something about her attitude toward the culture as a whole.) In effect, she is making a sociological statement in predominantly impressionistic terms. But in doing so, it seems to me, she is only partially successful. (Early in the essay Didion says: "We live entirely, especially if we are writers, by the imposition of a narrative line upon disparate images, by the 'ideas' with which we have learned to freeze the shifting phantasmagoria which is our actual experience" [p. 11]. What she has given us in "The White Album," however, is not a narrative line, but the "disparate images" and "shifting phantasmagoria" themselves. Although many interesting lines of development are suggested, none is really followed through.)[14]

I suspect that this essay would have been more effective had Didion's focus been less diffuse, had she not left us wanting to know so much more about the Fergusons and Linda Kasabian. To begin to appreciate the possibilities which go undeveloped here, one need only consider the author's brilliant treatment of the Lucille Miller murder case in "Some Dreamers of the Golden Dream" (*Slouching*, pp. 3–28). In that essay, unlike "The White Album," she does in fact impose narrative order upon the phantasmagoria of actual experience.

I do not mean to suggest that "The White Album" is without redeeming merit. Here, as elsewhere, Didion demonstrates a capacity for engaging our interest. (Indeed, her very stylistic virtues—by raising our expectations of everything she writes—can lead to unreasonable disappointment in work that is less than her best.) Unfortunately, she has allowed that interest to dissipate by sacrificing coherence for the sake of scope. Perhaps the only way to avoid such a pitfall is to find a story which can also serve as cultural synecdoche. The next essay to which we shall turn accomplishes that very task.

The title piece of *Slouching Towards Bethlehem* is one of Didion's most famous journalistic efforts. In addition to being a vivid and powerful depiction of life in Haight-Ashbury, it addresses itself as well to the cultural matrix from which Haight-Ashbury was spawned. As the author indicates in her preface, "I was talking about something more general than a handful of children wearing mandalas on their foreheads" (p. xiv). And yet, many readers missed all but the most obvious and tangential aspects of Didion's analysis.[15] (For some the essay's very timeliness may have obscured the broader thrust of its argument.)

Didion begins by describing the context of American culture in the mid-1960s. "The center was not holding," she writes. "It was a country of bankruptcy notices and public-auction announcements and commonplace reports of casual killings and misplaced children and abandoned homes and vandals who misspelled even the four-letter words they scrawled. It was a country in which families routinely disappeared, trailing bad checks and repossession papers. Adolescents drifted from city to torn city, sloughing off both the past and the future as snakes shed their skins, children who were never taught and would never now learn the games that had held the society together" (p. 84).

Most of the rest of this essay is devoted to an accumulation—a veritable montage—of short, fragmented scenes. Formalistically, its author is doing here what she would do in *Play It as It Lays* and *A Book of Common Prayer*: she shapes the printed page in such a way that its very appearance tells us something about her story. For the most part, "Slouching Towards Bethlehem" consists of a large number of relatively short paragraphs, quite a few shifts in scene, and very little overt narrative connection. Thus the reading experience itself conveys a sense of fragmentation. However, the general consistency of ambience and mood and Didion's own artistic control are so complete that these fragments form a larger mosaic; we are never lost in the incoherence of imitative form.

Although Didion is striving for cumulative effect, several individual descriptions and bits of dialogue are particularly memorable. One recalls, for example, Max and Sharon—a young couple who "plan to leave for Africa and India, where they can live off the land. 'I got this little trust fund, see,' Max says, 'which is useful in that it tells cops and border patrols I'm OK, but living off the land is the thing. You can get your high and get your dope in the city, OK, but we gotta get out somewhere and live organically'" (p. 96). Obviously Max and Sharon are not aware that Indians and Africans themselves find it difficult to live off the land, that the material largesse of America—which hippies supposedly repudiate—is frequently the only thing standing between these foreign peoples and mass starvation. But such considerations are too mundane to trouble the flower children; their minds are focused on more ethereal concerns. For example, a young man named Steve asserts: "I found love on acid. But I lost it. And now I'm finding it again. With nothing but grass" (p. 97).

One also recalls the terse clarity and laconic precision with which Didion describes a nonparticipant's view of an acid trip: "At three-thirty that afternoon," she writes, "Max, Tom, and Sharon placed tabs under their tongues and sat down together in the living room to wait for the flash. Barbara stayed in the bedroom, smoking hash. During the next four hours a window banged once in Barbara's room, and about five-thirty some children had a fight in the street. A curtain billowed in the afternoon wind. A cat scratched a beagle in Sharon's lap. Except for the sitar music on the stereo there was no other sound or movement until seven-thirty, when Max said 'Wow'" (p. 106).

And then there is the author's dispassionate account of the lives of Haight-Ashbury's youngest inhabitants. We read of a three-year-old named Michael who amuses himself by burning joss sticks and by sitting on a rocking horse whose paint has worn off. "The first time I ever saw Michael," Didion remembers, "was on that rocking horse, a very blond and pale and dirty child on a rocking horse with no paint. A blue theatrical spotlight was the only light in the Warehouse that afternoon, and there was Michael in it, crooning softly to the wooden horse. Michael is three years old. He is a bright child but does not yet talk" (p. 95). Another child—age five—is named Susan. When Didion encounters Susan the child is sitting "on the living-room floor, wearing a reefer coat, reading a comic book. She keeps licking her lips in concentration and the only off thing about her is that she's wearing white lipstick. . . . For a year now her mother has given her both acid and peyote. Susan describes it as getting stoned" (pp. 127, 128).

Finally, the last paragraph of "Slouching Towards Bethlehem" is eloquently symbolic, a veritable ideogram of the pathological self-absorption and moral disorder which pervade Haight-Ashbury:

Sue Ann's three-year-old Michael started a fire this morning before anyone was up, but Don got it out before much damage was done. Michael burned his arm though, which is probably why Sue Ann was so jumpy when she happened to see him chewing on an electric cord. "You'll fry like rice," she screamed. The only people around were Don and one of Sue Ann's macrobiotic friends and somebody who was on his way to a commune in the Santa Lucias, and they didn't notice Sue Ann screaming at Michael because they were in the kitchen trying to retrieve some very good Moroccan hash which had dropped down through a floorboard damaged in the fire. (p. 128)

Although one can hardly gainsay the praise this essay has received, it is nevertheless possible to suggest a few critical reservations. To begin with, Didion's objective, camera-eye narration may have drawbacks as well as advantages. Since the hippies all seem interchangeable, the accumulation of scene upon scene begins—after a while—to become repetitive. Also, the author's own sociological analysis, though discerning, is all too brief and incomplete. (Of course, when this essay first appeared—in 1967—the press was glutted with analyses of the hippie phenomenon.) Nor is it clear that Didion's insistence on keeping a low profile is altogether fortunate. She tells us that she wrote this essay at a time of personal distress, when her own center was not holding; yet her persona in the essay is virtually invisible, as if she were just another reporter or—in the argot of Haight-Ashbury—a "media poisoner."[16]

Ultimately, though, we must judge a writer's work by what is there, not by what might have been there. Perhaps we would even be wise to adopt a standard of literary affectiveness which Didion herself implies in the preface of *Slouching Towards Bethlehem*, where she tells us that certain lines from Yeats's "The Second Coming" "have reverberated in my inner ear as if they were surgically implanted there" (p. xiii). And the essay which derives its title from one of those lines assaults our memory with a remarkably similar tenacity.

CHAPTER 4

Democratic Vistas

WHEN future generations want to know what life was like in America during the 1960s and 70s, they will turn not to the fiction but to the journalism of our age. The writings of John McPhee, George Plimpton, Norman Mailer, Russell Baker, William F. Buckley, Gore Vidal, James Baldwin, Larry King, Tom Wolfe, John Gregory Dunne, David Halberstam, and others create a picture of our era which, in its own way, is just as authentic as the portrait of the 1920s given us by Hemingway and Fitzgerald. This picture would be incomplete, however, without the journalistic contributions of Joan Didion.[1]

In the preceding chapter we focused on the way in which Didion's essays serve to articulate her political and moral views, culminating with a look at the respective title pieces of her two volumes of collected essays. In this chapter we shall turn our attention to her treatmment of the ordinary manners and mores which help to define us as a people. First we will examine what she calls "the invisible city," that segment of the Southern California populace which lives on the fringes of society (not the poor or the dispossessed, but the lower middle class who subsist on various dreams of God, power, or Mammon). Then we shall scrutinize what the author has to say about America's largest but least fashionable minority group—the suburban middle class. But before doing either of those things, it might be useful for us to note what she has written about the practice of journalism itself.

It is not surprising that Didion—who has written so frequently and so perceptively about the craft of fiction—should also ponder the nature of that other genre at which she has toiled. Indeed, she does precisely that in "Alicia and the Underground Press" (*Saturday Evening Post*, January 13, 1968). Her discussion here begins with a rather disarming statement: "The only newspapers," she writes, "that do not leave me in the grip of a profound physical conviction that the oxygen has been cut off from my brain tissue, very probably by an Associated Press wire, are *The Wall Street Journal*, the *Los Angeles*

Free Press, the Los Angeles *Open City* and the *East Village Other*. . . . *The Wall Street Journal* talks to me directly (that I have only a minimal interest in much of what it tells me is beside the point), and so does the 'underground' press."[2] In effect, Didion is rejecting textbook notions of objectivity in favor of what has come to be called "advocacy journalism." "I admire objectivity very much," she continues, "but I fail to see how it can be achieved if the reader does not understand the writer's particular bias. For the writer to pretend that he has none lends the entire venture a mendacity that has never infected *The Wall Street Journal* and does not yet infect the underground press."

As an example of the sort of journalism she admires Didion cites "three lines of haiku-like perfection" in which a reader named Alicia tells the *Los Angeles Free Press* all she knows about the University of Michigan: "The professors and their wives are ex-Beatniks (Berkeley, Class of '57) and they go on peace marches and bring daffodils to U Thant. Some of the kids still believe in Timothy Leary and Kahlil Gibran. Some of their parents still believe in the Kinsey Report." Similarly, Joan Didion—ex-middle-class Protestant (Berkeley, Class of '56)—still believes that the art of moral journalism consists of telling the truth and of writing well. It is, like playing the dulcimer, a perishable art.

I   *The Invisible City*

The year is 1968 and Elder Robert J. Theobold, pastor of the Friendly Bible Apostolic Church—Port Hueneme, California—has received direct word from the Almighty of an impending earthquake. As a result, he and his followers plan to pull up stakes and relocate in Murfreesboro, Tennessee, an area of infrequent earth tremors. In the first section of a *White Album* sequence entitled "Notes Toward a Dreampolitik" Didion tells of her visit with Brother Theobold and his flock.

What she gives us in this essay is a slice of the exotic religious life of Southern California. In Nathanael West's *The Day of the Locust*, Evelyn Waugh's *The Loved One*, and dozens of other fictions we read of the various cults and sects which flourish out there in what Didion calls "the interior wilderness," where the actual wilderness has come to an end. And yet, these works are—if anything—less bizarre than the reality they are satirizing. (What novelist, for example, would have dreamed of Jim Jones and the People's Temple?) Didion is sensitive enough to the possibilities in her material not to strain for effect. Simply by allowing her subjects to speak for themselves she is able to achieve an ironic juxtaposition of the theological and the mundane.[3] Brother Theobold, for example, says to the author: "From the natural point of view I didn't care to go to Murfreesboro at all. . . . We just bought this place, it's the nicest place we ever had. But I put it up to the Lord, and the Lord said *put it up for sale.* Care for a Dr. Pepper?" (*Album*, p. 98).

When Didion enters this essay to speak in her own voice she comments perceptively on what the Pentecostal sects tell us about our culture. "In the social conventions by which we now live," she writes, "there is no category for people like Brother Theobold and his congregation, most of whom are young and white and nominally literate. . . . They participate in the national anxieties only through a glass darkly" (p. 98).

To an astonishing extent they keep themselves unviolated by common knowledge, by the ability to make routine assumptions; when Brother Theobold first visited Murfreesboro he was dumbfounded to learn that the courthouse there had been standing since the Civil War. "The *same building*," he repeated twice and then got out a snapshot as corroboration. In the interior wilderness no one is bloodied by history, and it is no coincidence that the Pentecostal churches have their strongest hold in places where Western civilization has its most superficial hold. There are more than twice as many Pentecostal as Episcopal churches in Los Angeles. (pp. 98–99)

In the next section of "Dreampolitik" Didion looks at a major element in the popular culture of another part of "the invisible city." Her focus here is on motorcycle exploitation films, or bike movies. She attended nine of these films during a single week in 1970 and concludes that they constitute "a kind of underground folk literature for adolescents" (p. 100). "I suppose I kept going to these movies," she writes, "because there on the screen was some news I was not getting from the *New York Times.* I began to think I was seeing ideograms of the future. To watch a bike movie is finally to appreciate the extent to which the toleration of small irritations is no longer a trait much admired in America, the extent to which a non-existent frustration threshold is seen not as psychopathic but as a 'right'" (pp. 100–101). Bike movies, in effect, play out endless variations on this alarming social phenomenon.

These films are insistently amoral and relentlessly the same: "There is always that instant in which the outlaw leader stands revealed as existential hero. There is always that 'perverse' sequence in which the bikers batter at some psychic sound barrier, degrade the widow, violate the virgin, defile the rose and the cross alike, break on through to the other side and find, once there, 'nothing to say'" (p. 100). Didion describes the audience for whom such fantasies are tailored as consisting of "boys who majored in shop and worked in gas stations and later held them up . . . , children of vague 'hill' stock who grow up absurd in the West and Southwest, children whose whole lives are an obscure grudge against a world they think they never made." "These children," she concludes, "are, increasingly, everywhere, and their style is that of an entire generation" (p. 101).

Dreams, however, do not need to be psychopathic. Even those fostered by the cinema can be remarkably benign. In continuing her look at the fringes of society, Didion focuses on one such benign dreamer—an unknown actress named Dallas Beardsley. In many ways Dallas is akin to the host of starstruck young characters who populate countless Hollywood novels (one thinks of Faye Greener and Tod Hackett in West's *The Day of the Locust*, of the marathon dancers in Horace McCoy's *They Shoot Horses, Don't They?* and of Mona Matthews and Ralph Carston in McCoy's *I Should Have Stayed Home*). Dallas is a twenty-two-year-old woman who has spent her entire life in Southern California, dreaming of motion picture fame. "There is no one like me in the world," she declares in a full-page advertisement on the fifth page of *Daily Variety*, "I'm going to be a movie star" (p. 102).

Upon reading Miss Beardsley's advertisement Didion reflects: "It seemed an anachronistic ambition, wanting to be a movie star; girls were not supposed to want that in 1968. . . . They were supposed to know that wanting things leads in general to grief, and that wanting to be a movie star leads in particular to U.C.L.A. Neuropsychiatric. Such are our conventions" (p. 102). But it would be difficult to convince Dallas Beardsley of this. When Didion asks her what it means to be a movie star, Dallas replies: "'It means being known all over the world. . . . And bringing my family a bunch of presents on Christmas Day, you know, like carloads, and putting them by the tree. And it means happiness, and living by the ocean in a huge house.' She paused. 'But being *known*. It's important to me to be *known*'" (p. 103). In a sense her dream life is Dallas Beardsley's most vivid reality.[4]

As she "drove home that day through the somnolent back streets of Hollywood," Didion "had the distinct sense that everyone I knew had some fever which had not yet infected the invisible city. In the invisible city girls were still disappointed at not being chosen cheerleader. In the invisible city girls still got discovered at Schwab's and later met their true loves at the Mocambo or the Troc, still dreamed of big houses by the ocean and carloads of presents by the Christmas tree, still prayed to be known" (p. 104).

Didion concludes her "Notes Toward a Dreampolitik" with a quick cinematic cut to a Gamblers Anonymous meeting in Gardena, California, "draw poker capital of Los Angeles County" (p. 104). Her description of this meeting is a shortened version of a February 10, 1968, *Saturday Evening Post* column entitled "Getting Serenity." That original column, it seems to me, was supercilious and elitist in tone. In effect, Didion was taking a cheap shot at some rather inarticulate but troubled people, compulsive gamblers who were trying to reform themselves through mutual self-help. However, in the revised version of this sketch, she eschews editorial comment; giving us instead only a *cinéma vérité* glimpse of the recovered gamblers. This latter approach is more effective, if only because it is less overtly snide and condescending.

In these four short pieces of prose that she has brought together Didion has taken us on a tour of a world that is not her own. The lower-middle-class inhabitants of Southern California are not the landed gentry of Sacramento or the beautiful people of Malibu. Neither are they the hippies of Haight-Ashbury or the crazed murderers of Cielo Drive. They are what, in another section of the country, might be called "poor white trash." They are people whom the media generally ignore.

The invisible city, then, is not an actual location so much as it is a matrix of social attitudes, a state of mind. If Didion approaches this state of mind rather obliquely in "Notes Toward a Dreampolitik," she discusses it much more directly in "Some Dreamers of the Golden Dream" (*Slouching*, pp. 3–28). Her emphasis here is on the sort of people who view Southern California with the same ingenuous optimism that Dallas Beardsley reserves for the movie industry. ("The future looks good in the golden land," she writes, "because no one remembers the past. Here is where the hot wind blows and the old ways do not seem relevant, where the divorce rate is double the national average and where one person in every thirty-eight lives in a trailer. Here is the last stop for all those who came from somewhere else, for all those who drifted away from the cold and the past and the old ways. Here is where they are trying to find a new life style, trying to find it in the only places they know to look: the movies and the newspapers" [p. 4].) One such person is Lucille Marie Maxwell Miller.

Born on January 17, 1930, in Winnipeg, Manitoba, Lucille is the only child of Seventh-Day Adventist schoolteachers, Gordon and Lily Maxwell. After spending one year at Walla Walla College in Washington, she marries a twenty-four-year-old dentist named Gordon ("Cork") Miller. They spend some time in Guam, where Cork finishes his army duty, and in a small town in Oregon, before moving to California in 1957. "By the summer of 1964 they had achieved the bigger house on the better street and the familiar accoutrements of a family on its way up: the $30,000 a year, the three children for the Christmas card, the picture window, the family room, the newspaper photographs that showed 'Mrs. Gordon Miller, Ontario Heart Fund Chairman . . .'" (pp. 8–9). Also, that summer the marriage was beginning to come apart.

The summer had started badly. In May Cork Miller had been hospitalized for a bleeding ulcer and had sunk into a deep depression. "He told his accountant that he was 'sick of looking at open mouths,' and had threatened suicide" (p. 9). On July 8 Lucille Miller had filed for divorce. "Within a month, however, the Millers seemed reconciled. They saw a marriage counselor. They talked about a fourth child. It seemed that the marriage had reached the traditional truce, the point at which so many resign themselves to cutting both their losses and their hopes" (p. 9).

On the night of October 7 as Lucille Miller is on her way home with some milk from a twenty-four-hour market, her 1964 Volkswagen comes to a sudden stop, catches fire, and begins to burn. When help finally arrives, an hour and fifteen minutes later, Lucille is sobbing and incoherent. Her husband had been asleep in the back of the Volkswagen. "'What will I tell the children, when there's nothing left, nothing left in the casket,' she cried. . . . 'How can I tell them there's nothing left?'" (p. 6).

Some 200 mourners arrive for the closed-casket funeral. They hear Elder Robert E. Denton of the Seventh-Day Adventist Church of Ontario say that for Gordon Miller there will be "no more death, no more heartaches, no more misunderstandings" (pp. 6–7). "A light rain fell, a blessing in a dry season, and a female vocalist sang 'Safe in the Arms of Jesus.' A tape recording of the service was made for the widow, who was being held without bail in the San Bernardino County Jail on a charge of first-degree murder" (p. 7).

Didion structures her treatment of this story thematically rather than chronologically. At the outset she describes the Southern California setting, narrates the basic circumstances of Cork Miller's death, and informs us of Lucille's incarceration. Only then does the author fill us in on Mrs. Miller's background and give us a more detailed account of the events of October 7, 1964. Afterwards, we see the prosecution's case unfolding as the assistant district attorney argues that Lucille Miller drugged her husband and set their car on fire in order to collect his insurance money. A plausible motive for such a crime emerges when it is established that Lucille had been involved in an extramarital affair with one of her neighbors. Indeed, this case has the makings of classic soap opera.

What Didion gives us, however, is anything but soap opera. Her style is so controlled and her tone so objective that one is apt to lose sight of the authorial presence altogether. Yet, a close reading of "Some Dreamers of the Golden Dream" reveals a number of rhetorical and narrative strategies. Consider, for example, the emphasis which Didion places on Lucille Miller's membership in the Seventh-Day Adventist Church. (Although this essay predates the one on Brother Theobold, the prominence of offbeat religious sects in Southern California had already been established by West, Waugh, and a host of lesser lights.) That affiliation, along with her non-California origins and her suburban life-style, make Lucille a virtual embodiment of the Sunbelt ethos.

Also, the very language of this story is carefully crafted. At times Didion's narrative voice verges on the neoclassical. To say that the Millers had resigned "themselves to cutting both their losses and their hopes" is to employ a zeugma worthy of Alexander Pope. The grace and urbanity of such language contrasts ironically with the middle-class vulgarity of the story it tells. And there are certain implicit themes which address themselves less to the reader's intellect than to his intuitive sensibility. The selection of names is just such a theme. Early in the story we learn that for new arrivals in California "all life's promise comes down to a waltz-length white wedding dress and the birth of a Kimberly or a Sherry or a Debbi" (p. 4). Several pages later Didion tells us that Lucille Miller's daughter was allowed to choose a name for her mother's new baby. "She named the baby Kimi Kai" (p. 26).

In addition, Didion employs a favorite technique of the impressionistic essayist. She interlaces her narrative with so many specific and objective facts that her critical opinions take on an air of authority by virtue of their context. In one sentence we will be told of both the divorce rate and the density of trailer homes in Los Angeles, and in the next we will encounter generalizations about the psychology of an entire class of people. The tone of voice is the same in each instance, and the reader tends to accept what is being said as incontrovertible fact.

Finally, Didion seems to possess an unerring sense for the right visual detail. We come away from her story remembering that the crowds trying to get into the courtroom would begin forming at 6 A.M., and that "college girls camped at the courthouse all night, with stores of graham crackers and No-Cal" (p. 20). We recall the scene in the courtroom when the guilty verdict is brought in. As Lucille Miller's friend Sandy Slagle screams hysterically at the jurors, "sheriff's deputies moved in . . . , each wearing a string tie that read '1965 SHERIFF'S RODEO'" (p. 25). And then there is jail—the California Institution for Women at Frontera:

Cattle graze across the road, and Rainbirds sprinkle the alfalfa. Frontera has a softball field and tennis courts, and looks as if it might be a California junior college, except that the trees are not yet high enough to conceal the concertina wire around the top of the Cyclone fence. On visitor's day there are big cars in the parking area, big Buicks and Pontiacs that belong to grandparents and sisters and fathers (not many of them belong to husbands), and some of them have bumper stickers that say "SUPPORT YOUR LOCAL POLICE." (p. 25)

What we have in "Some Dreamers of the Golden Dream" may well be a variation on a familiar type of "new journalism." We have heard much in the past ten to fifteen years about the "nonfiction novel." (One thinks of Truman Capote's *In Cold Blood* and of several books from the typewriters of Norman Mailer and Tom Wolfe.) But one rarely thinks of Joan Didion as working in this genre: her journalism, after all, consists of relatively short articles, while her book-length narratives are all works of fiction. And yet, in her account of the murder trial of Lucille Miller, Didion has given us literature as well as reportage. She has written what must be considered a nonfiction short story, an exercise of what Alfred Kazin—in another context— has called "the imagination of fact."[5]

II *No Dark or Bloodied Ground*

In an age when various minority groups finally have begun to establish their niche in American life and literature, the much-maligned suburban middle class is also coming into its own. (In the realm of fiction John Cheever and John Updike have long written with perception and sensitivity about the Anglo-Saxon Protestant experience.) At the same time public attention is gradually shifting away from the more fashionable minorities of the 1960s back toward the numerically dominant class of American society. Such political phenomena as the taxpayers' revolt and the backlash against affirmative action signify a "conservative" drift in national sentiment. So, too, does the nostalgia craze in popular culture. A prime example of this craze is a special issue of *Esquire* (December 1975) devoted almost entirely to "great American things." The prologue to this issue is written by Tom Wolfe and its various articles include "Mom," by Grace Paley; "The Flag," by Russell Baker; "Coca-Cola," by Jean Stafford; "Baseball," by Tom Wicker; "Acid Indigestion," by Art Buchwald; "TV," by Andy Warhol; "Viable Solutions," by Edwin Newman; "Bourbon," by Walker Percy; "The Corner Store," by Eudora Welty; and "The Shopping Center," by Joan Didion.

Didion's feature opens with a litany of familiar names and half-forgotten concepts, creating the cumulative effect of "found poetry":

They float on the landscape like pyramids to the boom years, all those Plazas and Malls and Esplanades. All those Squares and Fairs. All those Towns and Dales, all those Villages, all those Forests and Parks and Lands. Stonestown. Hillsdale. Valley Fair, Mayfair. Northgate, Southgate, Eastgate, Westgate. Gulfgate. They are toy garden cities in which no one lives but everyone consumes, profound equalizers, the perfect fusion of the profit motive and the egalitarian ideal, and to hear their names is to recall words and phrases no longer quite current. Baby Boom. Comsumer Explosion. Leisure Revolution. Do-It-Yourself Revolution, Backyard Revolution. Suburbia.[6]

As is the case with so many of her interests, Didion's fascination with shopping centers is existential as well as conceptual. While working for *Vogue* in New York during the mid-1950s, she took a correspondence course from the University of California in shopping-center theory. (Her grand scheme was to finance her writing by planning and running a center or two.) She tells us that a decade earlier, though, the shopping center had been more than a mere economic expedient. It had been part of a mythic landscape. During those postwar years of the late 1940s, "the frontier had been reinvented, and its shape was the subdivision, that new free land on which all settlers could recast their lives *tabula rasa*. For one perishable moment there the American idea seemed about to achieve itself via FHA housing and the acquisition of major appliances" (p. 181).

But now that the postwar boom has given way to the era of limits and the automobile has come more readily to represent a fifth mortgage than a fifth freedom, shopping centers have ceased to be the enchanted bazaars of democracy. For Didion they have been reduced to temporary, interchangeable havens from the burden of being oneself. "In each of them one moves for a while in an aqueous suspension not only of light but of judgment, not only of judgment but of 'personality.' One meets no acquaintances at the Esplanade. One gets no telephone calls at Edgewater Plaza" (p. 186).

Like the shopping center, the freeway symbolizes an ethos of economic growth and personal mobility. A mere artery in most places, it is the very jugular of transportation in Los Angeles County—the nation's most sprawling metropolitan area. In "Bureaucrats" (*Album*, pp. 79–85) an irate commuter named Joan Didion tilts her lance at the California state highway bureaucracy for its attempt to disrupt the rhythm of the freeway. The proximate cause of her ire is a traffic experiment called Diamond Lane. "All 'The Diamond Lane' theoretically involved was reserving the fast inside lanes on the Santa Monica [freeway] for vehicles carrying three or more people, but in practice this meant that 25 per cent of the freeway was reserved for 3 per cent of the cars" (p. 81).

The situation which Didion describes involves more than a mere case of traffic congestion. What is at issue is an ethic of "enlightened" manipulation versus one of personal autonomy. The planners in Sacramento are interested in conserving fuel and in reducing pollution; the individual driver is interested in getting where he wants to go as conveniently and expeditiously as possible. Didion might have explored the philosophical implications of this conflict a bit more fully. What, for example, does the Diamond Lane slowdown tell us about the feasibility of Luddite solutions to the problems of a technological society? Have California's countercultural bureaucrats simply miscalculated the effects of their policy or do they secretly believe that snarl is beautiful? Although Didion only touches on these issues, she does evoke something of the mystique and ritual of the freeway. (In so doing she calls to mind the compulsive freeway driving of Maria Wyeth in *Play It as It Lays*.) "Mere driving on the freeway," Didion writes, "is in no way the same as participating in it. . . . Actual participation requires a total surrender, a concentration so intense as to seem a kind of narcosis, a rapture-of-the-freeway. The mind goes clean. The rhythm takes over" (p. 83).

In "1950 Was More Than 20 Years Ago" (*Life*, January 30, 1970) Joan Didion is less interested in discussing specific cultural phenomena than in assessing the general obsolescence of middle-class values and traditions in contemporary America. The occasion for this article is the national congress of the U.S. Junior Chamber of Commerce being held at the Miramar Hotel in Santa Monica. It is "a relentless succession of keynote banquets and award luncheons and prayer breakfasts and outstanding-young-men forums."[7] Reflecting on the people who attend such meetings, Didion observes, "I was listening to a true underground, the voice of all those who have felt themselves not merely shocked but personally betrayed by the turn of recent history. Here were some people who had been led to believe that the future was always a rational extension of the past. . . . Of course they would not admit their inchoate fears that the world was not that way anymore, that we were looking now not at one another and our 'problems' but into a void as dark and clear as space."

Didion does not rail against the Babbittry of these people nor does she describe them in such a way that they make fools of themselves. (There is an ironic distance here, but it is somewhat narrower than in her story on nerve gas in Hermiston, Oregon.) Indeed, by the end of the essay she has become wistful and speculative and even identifies herself with the peculiar homelessness—if not the specific values—of these fugitives from history, these anachronistic purveyors of civic hope:

Late one afternoon I sat in the Miramar lobby, watching the rain fall and the steam rise off the heated pool outside and listening to a song called *Now Is the Hour* on the Muzak and to a couple of Jaycees discussing student unrest and whether the solution to that problem might not begin with on-campus Jaycee groups. I remember dancing to *Now Is the Hour* when I was in high school in Sacramento. . . . That was in the early '50s, and I had spent the past few days with a thousand people who wanted to believe that the difference between the early '50s and the early '70s was 20 years. In a way I wanted to believe it too, but the difference was a great deal more than that, and now was not the hour for any of us.

Whose hour it may be, come round at last, she does not say. But outside the confines of the Miramar the ceremonies of innocence are drowned; the sleepy optimism of the 1950s seems more than a little quixotic when all around us the world is vexed to nightmare.

CHAPTER 5

Selling Somebody Out[1]

"I T is the great word of the twentieth century," writes Norman Mailer. "If there is a single word our century has added to the potentiality of language, it is ego."[2] The plausibility of Mailer's assertion, it seems to me, is borne out by the cult of personality in American life.

Although this cult probably began with the advent of motion pictures, it has accelerated in the 1960s and 70s as the children of the postwar baby boom have supplied a natural market for the emerging media of television and rock music. Originally centered in the world of entertainment, this cult is sufficiently broad to encompass figures in such diverse fields as politics, sports, and finance. As religious and community life have come to be eroded and the family structure itself to be fragmented, Americans increasingly have focused their reverence on exemplars of worldly fame, wealth, and beauty. In the process, literature and the other traditional arts have been supplanted by popular culture. Indeed, whether the medium be celluloid, cathode rays, or electrified dissonance, the message is the same: our celebrities are our gods.[3]

Public fascination with culture heroes has created in its wake a whole genre of personality journalism. From Edward R. Murrow's "Person to Person" in the mid-1950s to *People* magazine in the mid-1970s, the broadcast and print media have sought to make our heroes more accessible to us, or at least to give us the impression of having done so. This effort, which is inherently neither praiseworthy nor censurable, has produced mixed results. At its worst personality journalism can be tawdry, sensational, and numbingly dull; but at its best it can suggest provocative social and philosophical insights. In the personality sketches written by Joan Didion these latter qualities tend to prevail.

I   *In the American Grain*

In her essay "7000 Romaine, Los Angeles 38" (*Slouching*, pp. 67–71) Didion writes about one of the most fascinating and enigmatic folk heroes in recent American history, Howard Hughes. A public man for much of his life, Hughes was a noted rake, a world-famous aviator, and—according to *Fortune*—"the proprietor of the largest pool of industrial wealth . . . under the absolute control of a single individual" (p. 69). He was also the romantic ideal of Joan Didion's youth.[4] Her essay, however, does not deal with the public Hughes. Just as he did not appear in public during the last years of his life, neither does he appear in "7000 Romaine." Instead of depicting the man himself, Didion presents us with "the folklore of Howard Hughes . . . , the way people react to him . . . , the terms they use when they talk about him" (p. 68). Her interest in the visible embodiments of the Hughes legend, she tells us, is similar to the fascination of Arthurian scholars with the Cornish coast.

7000 Romaine is a building owned by Hughes "in that part of Los Angeles familiar to admirers of Raymond Chandler and Dashiell Hammett: the underside of Hollywood, south of Sunset Boulevard, a middle-class slum of 'model studios' and warehouses and two-family bungalows" (p. 67). A locked building with an insincere WELCOME mat, 7000 Romaine is the "communications center" of the Hughes empire. Didion's essay, however, is not about this "communications center," or ultimately about Hughes himself, so much as it is about the mythopoeic sense of the American people. "That we have made a hero of Howard Hughes," she argues, "tells us something interesting about ourselves." It tells us that "the secret point of money and power in America is neither the things that money can buy nor power for power's sake . . . , but absolute personal freedom, mobility, privacy." "In a nation which increasingly appears to prize social virtues," she concludes, "Howard Hughes remains not merely antisocial but grandly, brilliantly, surpassingly, asocial. He is the last private man, the dream we no longer admit" (pp. 71, 72).

Although Georgia O'Keeffe is not a celebrity in the same sense that Howard Hughes was, she is a woman whom Didion greatly admires, one who exemplifies a character trait common to many of the author's culture heroes—uncompromising individualism. Didion begins her discussion of Miss O'Keeffe (*Album*, pp. 126–30) by recalling an afternoon spent with Quintana viewing a huge O'Keeffe canvas at the Chicago Art Institute. When her daughter asks her "who drew" the *Sky Above Clouds* canvas, Didion tells her; and Quintana replies, "I need to talk to her" (p. 126).

"My daughter," Didion observes, "was making, that day in Chicago, an entirely unconscious but quite basic assumption about people and the work they do. She was assuming that the glory she saw in the work reflected a glory in its maker, that the painting was the painter as the poem is the poet, that every choice one made alone— every word chosen or rejected, every brush stroke laid or not laid down—betrayed one's character. *Style is character*" (pp. 126–27). The peculiar quality of Georgia O'Keeffe's style and character, the author maintains, is a kind of hardness. It "has not been in our century a quality much admired in women, nor in the past twenty years has it even been in official favor for men" (p. 127). And yet, there is little doubt that Didion approves of this quality and that she admires Georgia O'Keeffe for possessing it.

A product of the Wisconsin prairie, Georgia O'Keeffe went east as a young woman and finally, at the age of twenty-four, headed back west—stopping first in Texas and later in New Mexico. (No doubt, from her own regional perspective, Didion sees O'Keeffe's identity as a westerner to be a point in her favor.) The author concludes her essay by quoting Miss O'Keeffe's reminiscence of those years she spent in Texas. As she and her sister Claudia walk toward the horizon, watching the evening star come out, Georgia observes, "That evening star fascinated me. . . . It was in some way very exciting to me." Claudia has a gun and as the sisters walk she throws bottles into the air and shoots them before they hit the ground. But Georgia has only the "walk into nowhere and the wide sunset space with the star." "In a way," Didion notes, "one's interest is compelled as much by the sister Claudia with the gun as by the painter Georgia with the star, but only the painter left us this shining record" (p. 130).

Another kind of shining record is left by the subject of Didion's affectionate tribute "John Wayne: A Love Song" (*Slouching*, pp. 29–41). Like Georgia O'Keeffe, Wayne is an individual for whom style and character are one. And even more than Howard Hughes, the Duke has been for Didion a lifelong figure of romance. The author's "love song" is structured symmetrically as it begins with a discussion of her childhood infatuation with Wayne, proceeds to give us a camera-eye view in prose of the Duke filming his one hundred sixty-fifth movie, and concludes by describing a dinner engagement among Wayne, an adult Didion, and their respective spouses. Although this shifting focus is only partially effective—the middle of the essay is perhaps disproportionately long—Didion has found in John Wayne something she has lacked in certain of her other essays: a subject commensurate with her ability to write about it.

In a sense, though, the author's subject is less an actual man than it is the ongoing relationship between herself and a mythic presence on the motion picture screen; a relationship which began in the summer of 1943 when she was eight years old. At that time her father was stationed at Peterson Field in Colorado Springs, a place which Didion remembers primarily for a hot wind which brought dust from Kansas and for the artificial blue rain behind the bar at the Officer's Club. Under these circumstances her only refuge from boredom lay in "the darkened Quonset hut which served as a theater" (p. 29), where three or four afternoons a week she and her brother sat on folding chairs watching movies. "It was there," she writes, "that summer of 1943 while the hot wind blew outside, that I first saw John Wayne. Saw the walk, heard the voice. Heard him tell the girl in a picture called *War of the Wildcats* that he would build her a house, 'at the bend in the river where the cottonwoods grow'" (pp. 29–30). The men whom Didion has known in the ensuing years have had many virtues, but "they have never been John Wayne, and they have never taken . . . [her] to that bend in the river where the cottonwoods grow." "Deep in that part of my heart where the artificial rain forever falls," she tells us, "that is still the line I wait to hear" (p. 30).

Didion's personal revelations take on added significance when one considers how many thousands, perhaps millions, of Americans can say with her that John Wayne "determined forever the shape of certain of our dreams" (p. 30). It was for this reason that the news of Wayne's lung cancer proved so traumatic.[5] The Duke's illness was an impingement of reality upon that dream world where nothing bad could happen. Thus it was with a certain foreboding that the author went to Mexico to observe Wayne filming *The Sons of Katie Elder*, the picture which "his illness had so long delayed" (p. 32). At this point Didion removes herself from the center of the essay and focuses instead upon the peculiarly male camaraderie which existed on the movie set among Wayne, Dean Martin, and director Howard Hathaway—down there in Durango, Mexico. Apparently, the conclusion we are to draw here is that the Duke had, in fact, "licked the big C" and that he was still the molder of dreams. This latter fact is amply demonstrated when, at the end of her essay, Didion tells us of the dinner which she and her husband shared with Wayne and his wife at an expensive restaurant their last week in Mexico.

Toward the end of a pleasant but ordinary evening "something happened." "Suddenly the room seemed suffused with the dream," Didion tells us, "and I could not think why. Three men appeared out of nowhere, playing guitars" (p. 41). Wayne orders more wine ("'Pouilly-Fuisse for the rest of the table . . . and some red Bordeaux for the Duke'") "and all the while the men with the guitars kept playing." Then Didion realizes "what they were playing, what they had been playing all along: 'The Red River Valley' and the theme from *The High and the Mighty*." "They did not quite get the beat right," she says, "but even now I can hear them, in another country and a long time later, even as I tell you this" (p. 41).

II   *Against the Grain*

We can infer from her admiration of Howard Hughes, Georgia O'Keeffe, and John Wayne that Didion prizes individualism quite highly. Even at her most conventional she is her own woman, and any attempt to pigeonhole her must be subject to considerable qualification. It would be wrong, however, to see her as a thoroughgoing iconoclast; for, even though individualism and iconoclasm frequently overlap, they are not the same thing. This distinction is borne out quite clearly in her respective discussions of Helen Gurley Brown, Joan Baez, and Bishop James Pike. Having achieved fame in the iconoclastic 1960s, each of these individuals represents a particular kind of dissent against traditional American values. In the lives of each we read parables of our time.

The first of these parables is "Bosses Make Lousy Lovers"[6] (*Saturday Evening Post*, January 30, 1965), the story of Helen Gurley Brown. Didion begins by tuning us in on an all-night radio talk show on an evening in which listeners debate two principal topics—the swimming ability of rattlesnakes and the cultural significance of Mrs. Brown. In addressing herself to the latter topic one caller maintains, "This *Sex for the Secretary* creature—whatever her name is— certainly isn't contributing anything to the morals in this country" (p. 34); while another listener contends that "Helen is one of the few authors trying to tell us what's really going *on*." ("Hefner's another," that caller adds, "and he's also controversial, working in, uh, another area" [p. 36].) According to Didion,

it is Helen Gurley Brown's peculiar destiny to call forth such voices in the night, every night, somewhere in these United States. There is a sense in which she has found, in the late-night and daytime talk shows, her predestined medium.... [Here she] reaches a twilight world of the lonely, the subliterate, the culturally deprived, gets in touch with people whose last contact with the printed and bound word was *Calories Don't Count*.... Her market seems to be composed of people who ordinarily set eyes on a book only when Johnny Carson holds one up. (p. 36)

To a large degree the risqué image of Helen Gurley Brown is a media creation, as is the controversy which surrounds her. Surpris-

ingly enough, she tends—even in her books—to be less concerned
with the erotic than with the domestic ("Mrs. Brown is forever nudg-
ing the reader out of bed and into the kitchenette") and her sensibility
has running through it "a thread of old-fashioned ambition so increasingly uncommon that . . . younger readers will recognize it only
from early Joan Crawford movies on the *Late Late Show*" (p. 36).
Helen Gurley Brown is actually "the small-town girl who wanted to
be the toast of Big Town" (p. 36). And by shrewdly fostering an avant-
garde persona, the author of *Sex and the Single Girl* realizes her
dream: she wins the least avant-garde of social distinctions—fame
and material success.

In "Where the Kissing Never Stops" (*Slouching*, pp. 42–60) Didion
writes about a very different kind of dissenter from the mainstream of
American values, Joan Baez. Here the author's attitude toward her
subject is evidently mixed. On the positive side she clearly seems to
respect Baez as a person (she identifies the singer's "most striking
characteristic" as "her absolute directness, her absence of guile" and
contends that Baez "is what used to be called a lady"[p. 44]).

Moreover, Didion seems mildly scornful of some of the singer's
more vindictive opponents—middle-class homeowners in Monterey
County who are attempting to close Baez's nearby Institute for the
Study of Nonviolence by contending that it is in violation of a clause
in the county zoning code "which prohibits land use 'detrimental to
the peace, morals, or general welfare of Monterey County'" (p. 42).
One such homeowner is a dentist's wife—Mrs. Gerald Petkuss—who
claims to have been plagued "by people associated with Miss Baez's
school coming up to ask where it was although they knew perfectly
well where it was." To emphasize her point Mrs. Petkuss adds, "One
gentleman I remember had a beard" (p. 43).

Didion's personal respect for Baez and her obvious disdain for the
philistianism of the Monterey County residents, however, does not
lead the author to an endorsement of Baez's school. For she is too
much of a political skeptic to be taken in by the ingenuous idealism of
the place. Such skepticism comes through in her description of the
school's students. They are, she tells us, "on the average very young,
very earnest, and not very much in touch with the larger scene, less
refugees from it than children who do not quite apprehend it" (p. 49).
Their belief in the practical efficacy of nonviolence, for example, is
more than a little naive: "they discuss a proposal from Berkeley for an
International Nonviolent Army: 'The idea is, we go to Vietnam and
we go into these villages, and then if they burn them, we burn too'"
(p. 49).

Although Didion does not explicitly compare Baez's school with the Garden of Eden, one comes away from her essay thinking of the Monterey County retreat as the moral equivalent of a germ-free environment. It is "a place where the sun shines and the ambiguities can be set aside a little while longer, a place where everyone can be warm and loving and share confidences" (p. 58). At the end of the day the students are reluctant about gathering up their belongings; "and by the time they are ready to leave Joan Baez is eating potato salad with her fingers from a bowl in the refrigerator, and everyone stays to share it, just a little while longer where it is warm" (p. 60).

If her view of Helen Gurley Brown and of Joan Baez could be defined as one of qualified admiration, Didion's opinion of the late Episcopal Bishop of California—James Albert Pike—is one of utter contempt.[7] Whereas Brown may remind the author of a Joan Crawford heroine and Baez may possess the aura of a guileless lady, Pike is an unambiguous reflection of much that is self-indulgent and meretricious in contemporary American culture. In her essay "James Pike, American" (*Album*, pp. 51–58), Didion makes this very point. "The man was a Michelin to his time and place," she writes.

At the peak of his career James Albert Pike carried his peace cross (he had put away his pectoral cross for the duration of the Vietnam war, which outlived him) through every charlatanic thicket in American life, from the Center for the Study of Democratic Institutions to the Aspen Institute of Humanistic Studies to Spiritual Frontiers, which was at the time the Ford Foundation of the spirit racket. James Albert Pike was everywhere at the right time. He was in Geneva for *Pacem in Terris*. He was in Baltimore for the trial of the Catonsville Nine, although he had to be briefed on the issue in the car from the airport. He was in the right room to reach his son, Jim Jr., an apparent suicide on Romilar, via seance. The man kept moving. (p. 57)

Pike was born in Oklahoma in 1913 and won first prize in the Better Babies Contest at the Oklahoma State Fair two years running. ("'I thought you would like that,'" his mother told his biographers "almost sixty years later, 'He started out a winner'" [p. 53].) After the death of his father, Pike with his mother moved to California, where young James was raised a Roman Catholic. At the age of eighteen, however, he became an agnostic and remained one through his college years at UCLA. He later went east to attend Yale Law School and subsequently to work for the Securities and Exchange Commission in Washington. At that time he wrote to his mother: "Practically every churchgoer you meet in our level of society is Episcopalian, and an R.C. or straight Protestant is as rare as hen's teeth" (p. 54). Didion comments on this letter:

One thinks of Gatsby coming up against the East. One also thinks of Tom Buchanan and his vast carelessness (some 25 years later in Santa Barbara, when the Bishop of California's mistress swallowed 55 sleeping pills he appears to have moved her from his apartment into her own before calling an ambulance and to have obscured certain evidence before she died), or even of Dick Diver, who also started out a winner, and tried to embrace the essence of the American continent in Nicole as James Albert Pike would now try to embrace it in the Episcopal Church. *Practically every churchgoer you meet in our level of society is Episcopalian.* (pp. 54–55)

The author makes several other comparisons between Pike and various Fitzgerald characters. (She cites, for example, Nick Caraway's famous line: "Tom and Gatsby, Daisy and Jordan and I, were all westerners, and perhaps we possessed some deficiency in common which made us subtly unadaptable to Eastern life.") Indeed, she finds emerging from Pike's biography "the shadow of a great literary character, a literary character in the sense that Howard Hughes and Whittaker Chambers were literary characters, a character so ambiguous and driven and revealing of his time and place that his gravestone in the Protestant cemetery in Jaffa might well have read only JAMES PIKE, AMERICAN" (p. 53). And quite appropriately, Pike's death is itself a sort of literary metaphor, as he departed this mortal life in a canyon near the Dead Sea in search of the historic Jesus. "Five years after he finished [constructing] Grace [Cathedral] James Albert Pike left the Episcopal Church altogether, detailing his pique in the pages of *Look*, and drove into the Jordanian desert in a white Ford Cortina rented from Avis. He went with his former student and bride of nine months, Diane. Later she would say that they wanted to experience the wilderness as Jesus had. They equipped themselves for this mission with an Avis map and two bottles of Coca-Cola" (p. 52).

Although he was an indifferent scholar, Pike's celebrity status placed him in the forefront of the radical theology of the 1960s. American culture was permeated at that time with a kind of secular millennialism, a desire—in Eric Voegelin's phrase—to "immanentize the eschaton."[8] As a sort of corollary to this development, many theologians sought to make their faith less supernatural and more "relevant" to the nonreligious world. These were years of demythologizing, years when an entire theological movement would proclaim the "death of God." (Pike didn't go quite that far; he still spoke of God, but when he did so—Didion tells us—it was because he had "streamlined the Trinity, eliminating the Son and the Holy Ghost" [p. 51].) In short, these were years when men in their arrogance and their naiveté were busy remaking things in Heaven and on Earth. And to Didion's mind these "were the years for which James Albert Pike was born." She tells us that "when the man who started out a winner was lying dead in the desert his brother-in-law joined the search party, and prayed for the assistance of God, Jim Jr., and Edgar Cayce." "I think," Didion concludes, "I have never heard a more poignant trinity" (p. 58).[9]

CHAPTER 6

Some Places of the Mind

E VERY schoolboy knows that a work of fiction consists, among
other things, of plot, characterization, point of view, and setting.
It is somewhat more difficult, however, to say how these various
elements ought to work together. (One can intuitively know the
difference between a Greek tragedy and a soap opera without being
able to articulate that difference.) Since a work of art is frequently
either more or less than the sum of its parts, it is important for the
critic to see his task as ultimately one of holistic judgment and
interpretation. Nevertheless, the various disciplines of technique are
the means through which an artist fashions that work which is finally
the critic's focus of attention. Ideally, it should be possible to examine
these disciplines and yet avoid the pitfalls of reductive analysis.
Indeed, in approaching the superbly crafted fiction of Joan Didion, it
is essential that we maintain just such a critical balance.

In the following chapters we will look rather closely, and one
would hope comprehensively, at Didion's novels and short stories;
however, before doing so, it might be useful to examine a characteristic which distinguishes almost all of her writing and which cuts across
the various genres at which she has worked. I am thinking of her
ability to evoke a particular setting, to realize a palpable local ambience. Clearly, Didion believes that place is not just a physical
entity, but also a matrix for emotional associations; it is the frame of
reference within which one begins to know oneself and the world in
which one lives. (Accordingly, a major section of *Slouching Towards
Bethlehem* is entitled "Seven Places of the Mind.")

Because the relation between feeling and setting is less complex in
Didion's essays than in her fiction, those essays probably would be an
instructive point of departure for our consideration of their author's
affinity for place.[1] Therefore, in the next few pages, we will look at
several prose sketches which focus on a wide range of locations (both
on the American continents and in that Mid-Pacific place of the
mind—the Hawaiian Islands). As we ponder the geographical variety
of these locations, we might keep in mind an observation of Eudora

Welty's: "One place comprehended," she writes, "can make us understand other places better. Sense of place gives equilibrium; extended, it is sense of direction too. Carried off we might be in spirit, and should be, when we are reading or writing something good; but it is the sense of Place going with us still that is the ball of golden thread to carry us there and back and in every sense of the word to bring us home" ("Place in Fiction," pp. 128–29).

I   *Where Alph the Sacred River Ran*[2]

In her essays on William Randolph Hearst's San Simeon, on the new California governor's mansion, and on the J. Paul Getty museum Didion seems to be saying that the edifices which men erect can be seen as moral microcosms. Like a work of literature a man-made place makes a statement and tells a story. The emotions and attitudes which are aroused and nurtured by a private home, a public residence, or an art museum can tell us something about the respective sensibilities which prompted construction of these buildings, not to mention the society in which said buildings stand. Ultimately, however, Didion's discussion of California landmarks is less aesthetic or sociological than it is personal. Her encounter with these places becomes an occasion for self-revelation; and the revelation itself, a way of saying "I."

The first of the three essays mentioned above is called "A Trip to Xanadu" (*Saturday Evening Post*, September 21, 1968). By using this title Didion reminds us of Orson Welles's cinematic version of the story of William Randolph Hearst. In Welles's legendary film *Citizen Kane*, a newspaper publisher who resembles Hearst builds Xanadu, a palatial estate which is in many ways as rarefied as the dream-castle of Coleridge's poem. Describing the real-life Xanadu, Didion writes:

San Simeon was . . . exactly the castle a child would build, if a child had $220 million and could spend $40 million of it on a castle: a sand castle, an implausibility, a place swimming in warm golden light and theatrical mists, a pleasure dome decreed by a man who insisted, out of the dark fear we all know about, that all the surfaces be gay and brilliant and playful. . . . The leaves never fell at San Simeon, nothing went bare or died. All year long the roses and the fuchsia and the bougainvillea blossomed, half a million gallons of water glittered in the great pools, zebras and eland roamed the golden hills. The carillon bells could be heard for thirty miles. Brilliant Sienese flags fluttered over the long refectory dining tables. The guests ate pressed duck and wiped their hands on paper napkins: again, a child's fantasy, every meal a picnic.[3]

During her childhood Didion's fascination with San Simeon was due largely to its inaccessibility. As long as it was Hearst's private fantasy world, it possessed for her an aura of mystery. But when it became a public monument, a tourist site, Xanadu ceased any longer to be Xanadu. In touring the Hearst home as an adult, Didion took a child with her—a niece from Connecticut. The young girl liked this public monument well enough, liked its flowers, pools, and ornate ceilings; but her aunt reflects as they leave that the child "would have found it more affecting had she only glimpsed it from Highway 1, the gates barred, the castle floating in the distance. Make a place available to the eyes, and in certain ways it is no longer available to the imagination."

In "Many Mansions" (*Album*, pp. 67–73) Didion writes about a home which, unlike San Simeon, became a public monument without ever having been inhabited. It is the new California governor's mansion, the house that Ronald Reagan built and that Jerry Brown refuses to enter. In considering that house it might be interesting to keep the following description in mind: the "door was of gumwood painted like fumed oak and it hung on enormous hinges. Although made by machine, the hinges had been carefully stamped to appear hand-forged. The same kind of care and skill had been used to make the roof thatching, which was not really straw but heavy fire-proof paper colored and ribbed to look like straw."[4] The house being described here is not the new governor's mansion but Homer Simpson's bungalow in Nathanael West's *The Day of the Locust*; however, the same principle of tawdry artifice that West so brilliantly satirized in the 1930s is evident today in the "official residence" of California's chief executive: "The walls 'resemble' local adobe," Didion writes, "but they are not:

they are the same concrete blocks, plastered and painted a rather stale yellowed cream, used in so many supermarkets and housing projects and Coca-Cola bottling plants. The doorframes and the exposed beams "resemble" native redwood, but they are not: they are construction-grade lumber of indeterminate quality, stained brown. . . . [The house is] a monument not to colossal ego but to a weird absence of ego, a case study in the architecture of limited possibilities, insistently and malevolently "democratic," flattened out, mediocre and "open" and as devoid of privacy or personal eccentricity as the lobby area in a Ramada Inn. (pp. 68, 69)

"Many Mansions," however, is not simply a putdown of Governor Reagan's tastes. As with so many of Didion's writings about California, we have here a juxtaposition of the old with the new. As an adolescent, Joan Didion was familiar with the old governor's mansion. She was a high-school classmate of Earl Warren's daughter Nina and she used to visit the old mansion when Warren was governor. It was then her "favorite house in the world and probably still is":

[Its] bedrooms are big and private and high-ceilinged and [unlike those in the new mansion] they do not open on the swimming pool and one can imagine reading in one of them, or writing a book, or closing the door and crying until dinner.... There are hallways wide and narrow, stairs front and back, sewing rooms, ironing rooms, secret rooms.... In the kitchen there is no trash compactor and there is no "island" with the appliances built in but there are two pantries, and a nice old table with a marble top for rolling out pastry and making divinity fudge and chocolate leaves. (pp. 71, 72)

Didion's mixture of sophisticated commentary and wistful reminiscence ultimately tells us as much about her own rhetorical strategy as it does about the two houses she describes. By projecting a complex and engaging persona she lures us into accepting her aesthetic judgments as being inevitably those of the ideally sensitive observer. She uses her wit to grab our attention and to make her point, but leaves us with the impression that she is not merely glib, that she cares deeply about what she is saying. Such a strategy amounts to a delicate balancing act. In "Many Mansions" it is an act that works.

If "A Trip to Xanadu" is primarily lyrical in tone and "Many Mansions" a blend of polemicism and nostalgia, "The Getty" (*Album*, pp. 74–78) is mainly descriptive and speculative. Essentially, Didion is trying to understand the cultural significance of an art museum endowed by the late J. Paul Getty, to comprehend the statement that it makes and the varied response it elicits. Why does the art establishment disdain the Getty and why does the public like it? What ironic bond unites the sensibility of a dead billionaire with that of the American masses?

To begin with, Didion argues that the Getty makes a critically unfashionable statement about the nature of art and—hence—of life itself. It tells us

that the past was perhaps different from the way we like to perceive it. Ancient marbles were not always attractively faded and worn. Ancient marbles once appeared just as they appear here: as strident, opulent evidence of imperial power and acquisition. Ancient murals were not always bleached and mellowed and "tasteful." Ancient murals once looked as they do here: as if dreamed by a Mafia don. Ancient fountains once worked and drowned out that very silence we have come to expect and want from the past. Ancient bronze once gleamed ostentatiously. The old world was once discomfitingly new, or even nouveau, as people like to say about the Getty. (p. 76)

In effect, Didion sees an essential conflict between the pseudo-populism of most art critics and the basic conservatism of the actual public. If the critics believe that art should be fun and should serve as a catalyst to the untutored imagination, the public tends to prefer art that is both remote and "edifying." The Getty was built for just such a public. Indeed, "there is one of those peculiar social secrets at work here. On the whole 'the critics' distrust great wealth, but 'the public' does not. On the whole 'the critics' subscribe to the romantic view of man's possibilities, but 'the public' does not. In the end the Getty stands above the Pacific Coast Highway as one of those odd monuments, a palpable contract between the very rich and the people who distrust them least" (p. 78).

II *Where No One Is*

In "Rock of Ages" (*Slouching*, pp. 205–208) we move away from the relatively accessible and public world of San Simeon, the governor's mansions, and the Getty museum into an abandoned and decaying structure, a fortress sitting off the coast of California, the remnant of what used to be the federal prison at Alcatraz. Although that prison ceased to function on March 21, 1963, its ruins and the surrounding island endure—vestigial remains which are, to a certain sensibility, quaintly inviting. "It is not an unpleasant place to be," Didion writes, "out there on Alcatraz with only the flowers and the wind and a bell buoy moaning and the tide surging through the Golden Gate, but to like a place like that you have to want a moat" (p. 205).

The occasion for this essay is a trip the author made to the virtually deserted island described above. Here she tells of the present state of the prison building and of the life-style of the government employees who now guard this historic piece of federal property. Ever the clear-eyed observer, Didion gives us an interesting and seemingly objective report of what she sees. However, beneath the surface and between the lines of that report, there emerges the image of a woman who—by her own admission—at times does want a moat. Indeed, that aspect of her psyche which is touched by Alcatraz is suggested by the very title of her essay. Didion has appropriated a line from the famous hymn by Augustus Toplady, a line which in context reads: "Rock of ages, cleft for me, let me hide myself in thee."[5] For Didion the rock of Alcatraz—not Toplady's rock of faith—comes to embody the allure of security and isolation.

Although she does not depict the life that is led by the couple who serve as caretakers for the island as being totally idyllic, neither does Didion find it altogether unappealing. "Once a week the Harts take their boat to San Francisco to pick up their mail and shop at the big Safeway in the Marina, and occasionally Marie Hart gets off the island to visit her children. She likes to keep in touch with them by telephone, but for ten months recently, after a Japanese freighter cut the cable, there was no telephone service to or from Alcatraz. Every morning the KGO traffic reporter drops the *San Francisco Chronicle* from his helicopter, and when he has time he stops for coffee" (p. 206).

The sense of timelessness which isolation breeds is reinforced by the prison itself: "The buildings seem quite literally abandoned. The key locks have been ripped from the cell doors and the big electrical locking mechanisms disconnected. The tear-gas vents in the cafeteria are empty and the paint is buckling everywhere, corroded by the sea air, peeling off in great scales of pale green and ocher" (p. 207). Didion tells us of standing in a cell next to a makeshift calendar, "the months penciled on the wall with the days scratched off, May, June, July, August of some unnumbered year" (p. 208).

There is also a pervasive irony in an abandoned prison. When Alcatraz was in operation, its full resources were devoted to keeping prisoners in; now that there are no more prisoners, the government is interested only in keeping intruders out. As a more or less authorized intruder, Didion tells us that she "tried to imagine the prison as it had been, with the big lights playing over the windows all night long and the guards patrolling the gun galleries and the silverware clattering into a bag as it was checked in after meals, tried dutifully to summon up some distaste, some night terror of the doors locking and the boat pulling away" (p. 208). But her imagination fails her, or perhaps it leads in other directions. She likes it there on Alcatraz and she says of her return to the mainland, "I could tell you that I came back because I had promises to keep, but maybe it was because nobody asked me to stay" (p. 208).[6]

Something of the same sense of womblike security which the author feels at Alcatraz characterizes her response to another western landmark—Hoover Dam. In her essay "At the Dam" (*Album*, pp. 198–201) Didion finds herself in touch with a natural element which is austerely indifferent to human concerns. Her preoccupation here is not with water in its original power and beauty, but as it is harnessed by the artifice of technology. And her attitude toward this harnessing is complex if not downright ambivalent. (While she is not mounting a Luddite attack on the ravages of Leviathan, neither is she hymning a Randian panegyric to the glories of the machine age. Instead, Didion seems to accept the dam as being as much a part of the natural landscape as any work of God.)

In a sense the phenomenon which she is describing is an idea as well as a physical reality. It is the "showpiece of the Boulder Canyon project, the several million tons of concrete that made the Southwest plausible, the *fait accompli* that was to convey, in the innocent time of its construction, the notion that mankind's brightest promise lay in American engineering" (p. 199). The dam can be seen as "a monument to a faith since misplaced." Its bronzed sculptures "evoke muscular citizens of a tomorrow that never came, sheaves of wheat clutched heavenward, thunderbolts defied. Winged Victories guard the flagpole. The flag whips in the canyon wind. An empty Pepsi-Cola can clatters across the terrazzo. The place is perfectly frozen in time" (p. 199).

A nearly mystical reverence informs Didion's attitude toward the dam. She tells us that she now thinks of it "at times and in places where I once thought of the Mindanao Trench, or of the stars wheeling in their courses, or of the words *As it was in the beginning, is now and ever shall be, world without end, amen*" (p. 198). Indeed, there is something strangely comforting about the engulfing power of this place. When the emotional pressure becomes too great for Maria in *Play It as It Lays,* she goes out to Hoover Dam to be enraptured by the torrents surging around her: "She wanted to stay in the dam, lie on the great pipe itself, but reticence saved her from asking."[7]

Perhaps what is at work here is a desire to transcend the mutable by losing oneself in the eternal, or at least in something more permanent than any of our mortal lives. It is a desire—and a vanity—as old as the Tower of Babel. Didion begins to recognize the force of this desire when she is shown a star map which fixes the date on which the dam was dedicated. She speaks to the Reclamation man who tells her that this map was "for when we were all gone and the dam was left." "I had not thought much of it when he said it," she writes, "but I thought of it then, with the wind whining and the sun dropping behind a mesa with the finality of a sunset in space. Of course that was the image I had seen always, seen it without quite realizing what I saw, a dynamo finally free of man, splendid at last in its absolute isolation, transmitting power and releasing water to a world where no one is" (p. 201).

"It had rained in Los Angeles until the cliff was crumbling into the surf and I did not feel like getting dressed in the morning, so we decided to go to Mexico, to Guaymas, where it was hot. We did not go for marlin. We did not go to skin-dive. We went to get away from ourselves, and the way to do this is to drive, down through Nogales some day when the pretty green places pall and all that will move the imagination is some place difficult, some desert" (*Slouching*, p. 214). Thus Didion introduces us to the short but evocative prose sketch "Guaymas, Sonora."

As she continues to tell us of her trip, her descriptions of the Mexican countryside are rendered vivid by a clear, supple prose, almost hypnotic in its simplicity. Like Hemingway, Didion eschews heavy subordination and relies instead on a loose, expansive sentence structure—simple clauses strung together with coordinating conjunctions. Slipping easily from the past to the present tense, she puts us into the automobile with her as she makes her trip south:

After Nogales on Route 15 there is nothing but the Sonoran desert, nothing but mesquite and rattlesnakes and the Sierra Madre floating to the east, no trace of human endeavor but an occasional Pemex truck hurtling north and once in a while in the distance the dusty Pullman cars of the Ferrocarril del Pacifico. Magdalena is on Route 15, and then Hermosillo. . . . There is an airport in Hermosillo, and Hermosillo is only eighty-five miles above Guaymas, but to fly is to miss the point. The point is to become disoriented, shriven, by the heat and the deceptive perspectives and the oppressive sense of carrion. The road shimmers. The eyes want to close. (pp. 214–15)

What is happening to Didion as the protagonist of this sketch is a small-scale version of what happens to a number of characters in American literature. She leaves civilization, enters the wilderness, and returns different from when she left. (Whether we think of Thoreau at Walden Pond, of Huck on the Mississippi, or of Hemingway's Nick Adams by the two-hearted river, we see a consistent image of nature healing the perturbed spirit.) For the American hero does not remain permanently in the wilderness; instead, he withdraws from civilization to make the secular equivalent of a religious retreat, of Christ's forty days in the Judean desert. The journey is over only when he returns from the wilds. (Even Melville's Tommo risks his life to escape from "paradise" among the Typee.)

Similarly, Didion and her husband can remain only so long in the physical and emotional torpor of Guaymas, Sonora. "For a week we lay in hammocks," she writes, "and fished desultorily and went to bed early and got up very brown and lazy. My husband caught eight sharks, and I read an oceanography textbook, and we did not talk much. At the end of the week we wanted to do something, but all there was to do was visit the tracking station for an old space program or go see John Wayne and Claudia Cardinale in *Circus World*, and we knew it was time to go home" (p. 216).

III   *Earthly Cities*

With the essays "In Bogotá" (*Album*, pp. 187–97), "Seacoast of Despair," and "Marrying Absurd" (*Slouching*, pp. 209–13 and 79–83, respectively) Didion returns to civilization, to the cities that men build and the institutions they create. In the first of these essays she takes us close to the Equator, near the mythical republic of Boca Grande, to the Colombian capitol of Bogotá. She tells us that she had been on the coast, in Cartegena, until the allure of Bogotá became irresistible: "In Bogotá it would be cool," she writes. "In Bogotá one could get the *New York Times* only two days late and the *Miami Herald* only one day late and also emeralds, and bottled water. In Bogotá there would be fresh roses in the bathrooms at the Hotel Tequendama and hot water twenty-four hours a day and numbers to be dialed for chicken sandwiches from room service" (p. 187). She continues:

Maybe that is the one true way to see Bogotá, to have it float in the mind until the need for it is visceral, for the whole history of the place has been to seem a mirage, a delusion on the high savannah, its gold and its emeralds unattainable, inaccessible. . . . There on the very spine of the Andes gardeners espalier roses on embassy walls. Swarms of little girls in proper navy-blue school blazers line up to enter the faded tent of a tatty traveling circus: the elephant, the strong man, the tattooed man from Maracaibo. (p. 188)

Like much of South America, Bogotá represents a mix of cultures—including various indigenous, North American, and European traditions. Didion comes into contact with all three. When visiting the Gold Museum of the Banco de la República, for example, she thinks "of the nights when the Chibcha Indians lit bonfires on the Andes and confirmed their rulers at Guatavita" (pp. 188–89). The author quotes anthropologist Olivia Vlahos, who describes how the prospective ruler would step into the firelight, his naked body covered with resin. Priests would spread gold dust on the resin until the royal figure "'*gleamed like a golden statue.*'" Then the monarch-to-be stepped onto a raft "'*which was cut loose to drift into the middle of the lake. Suddenly he dived into the black water. When he emerged, the gold was gone, washed clean from his body. And he was king*'" (p. 189).

The influence of *norteamericana* (or U.S.) culture is a bit more immediate; though even here a "slight but definite dislocation of time" (p. 190) is evident. (The movie theaters—in 1973—are showing U.S. films from the mid-1960s and "the English-language racks of paperback stands were packed with Edmund Wilson's *The Cold War and the Income Tax*, the 1964 Signet edition" [p. 190].) The Americans staying in Bogotá convene at the U.S. embassy and in their dealings with the native population take pains to be inoffensive. (Didion tells us of an American actor who took cold showers for two weeks before realizing that the hot and cold taps in his room had been reversed. "He had never asked, he said, because he did not want to be considered an arrogant *gringo*" [p. 192].)[8]

Our final image of Bogotá is of Didion eating lunch in "the chilly dining room of the Hostería del Libertador" after coming up from a cathedral built deep in a Colombian salt mine. ("One could think of Chibcha sacrifices here, of the *conquistador* priests struggling to superimpose the European mass on the screams of the slaughtered children"; but, since the cathedral was built by the Banco de la República in 1954, one would be wrong [pp. 195–96].) She describes the elaborate "battery of silverplated flatware and platters and *vinaigrette* sauceboats" and the equally elaborate battery of waiters; "little boys, twelve or thirteen years old, dressed in tailcoats and white gloves and taught to serve as if this small inn on an Andean precipice were Vienna under the Hapsburgs" (p. 196).

The author watches one of these young waiters in white gloves as he picks up an empty wine bottle, fits it precisely into a wine holder, and proceeds into the kitchen—marching stiffly, "glancing covertly at the *maitre d'hotel* for approval." "It seemed to me later," Didion concludes, "that I had never before seen and would perhaps never again see the residuum of European custom so movingly and pointlessly observed" (p. 197).

The residuum of a very different kind of culture can be found in the Newport, Rhode Island, homes of some celebrated turn-of-the-century robber barons. And it is to this different culture that Didion turns her attention in "Seacoast of Despair." Here she argues that the opulence and ugliness of these Newport homes constitute a lesson in American social history. "No aesthetic judgment could conceivably apply to the Newport of Bellevue Avenue," she writes, "to those vast follies behind their handwrought gates; they are products of the metastasis of capital, the Industrial Revolution carried to its logical extreme, and what they suggest is how recent are the notions that life should be 'comfortable,' that those who live it should be 'happy'" (p. 210).

"Happiness [she continues] is, after all, a consumption ethic, and Newport is the monument of a society in which production was seen as the moral point, the reward if not exactly the end, of the economic process. . . . In Newport the air proclaims only the sources of money. Even as the sun dapples the great lawns and the fountains plash all around, there is something in the air that has nothing to do with pleasure and nothing to do with graceful tradition, a sense not of how prettily money can be spent but of how harshly money is made. (pp. 210, 211)

Although Newport is located on the Atlantic coast Didion understands the social and economic forces at work here in terms of her own peculiarly western sensibility. For example, she makes a useful contrast between San Simeon and the mansions of Newport. If the former embodies a Romantic view of human possibilities, the latter are decidedly Calvinist in tone. ("It is hard for me to believe," she writes, "that Cornelius Vanderbilt did not sense, at some point in time, in some dim billiard room of his unconscious, that when he built 'The Breakers' he damned himself [p. 212].) And yet, if Newport has none of the expansiveness of the West, it does possess the kind of masculine stridency which Didion sees as characteristic of the frontier. For this reason she can say that "Newport is . . . closer in spirit to Virginia City than to New York, to Denver than to Boston" (p. 211).

The author concludes her analysis by arguing that Newport is finally "homiletic, a fantastically elaborate stage setting for an American morality play in which money and happiness are presented as antithetical. . . . [Indeed,] the lesson of Bellevue Avenue is more seriously radical than the idea of Brook Farm. Who could fail to read the sermon in the stones of Newport? Who could think that the building of a railroad could guarantee salvation, when there on the lawns of the men who built the railroad nothing is left but the shadows of migrainous women, and the pony carts waiting for the long-dead children?" (pp. 212, 213).

If Newport represents the denouement of the American Dream—

the triumph of memory over hope—then Las Vegas is the future realized, an ambience wrenched out of time and removed from the matrix of ordinary human desire. In commenting on this town Didion writes: "I have never understood why the point . . . [of going there] is believed to be money, when the place is in fact profoundly immaterial, all symbol, all light and shadow and metaphor, a tableau vivant of lust and greed. I know Las Vegas to be a theater dedicated to the immediate gratification of every impulse, but I also know it to be a theater designed to numb those very impulses it promises to gratify."[9] Vegas is an oxymoronic city in which the distinctions between East and West, wilderness and civilization, and—indeed—illusion and reality are perpetually blurred. Nowhere, however, is the surrealism of this place more evident than in the industry described in "Marrying Absurd."

In Las Vegas, Clark County, Nevada—Didion tells us—it is possible to get married on the spot at almost any time, day or night. Alone among the fifty states Nevada "demands neither a premarital blood test nor a waiting period before or after the issuance of a marriage license. Driving in across the Mojave from Los Angeles, one sees the signs way out on the desert, looming up from that moonscape of rattlesnakes and mesquite, even before the Las Vegas lights appear like a mirage on the horizon: 'GETTING MARRIED? Free License Information First Strip Exit'" (p. 79).

Between 9:00 P.M. and midnight August 26, 1965, a record 171 couples plighted their respective troths in Las Vegas's assembly-line marriage parlors. (This otherwise unremarkable Thursday happened to be the last day that one could improve his draft status simply by getting married.) Sixty-seven of these couples were united by a single justice of the peace, Mr. James A. Brennan. "Mr. Brennan did one wedding at the Dunes and the other sixty-six in his office, and charged each couple eight dollars. One bride lent her veil to six others. 'I got it down from five to three minutes,' Mr. Brennan said later of his feat. 'I could've married them *en masse*, but they're people, not cattle. People expect more when they get married'" (p. 80).

In "Marrying Absurd" the narrator virtually disappears. No autobiographical recollection personalizes the sketch and no complex argument demands our assent. What we have instead is a series of starkly objective vignettes. In effect, Didion's material judges itself. Consider, for example, our final glimpse of love on the neon desert. A wedding party consisting of the bride, her parents, and her new husband sits in a Strip restaurant. The bride still wears her gown, and her mother, a corsage. A bored waiter pours pink champagne—

"on the house"—for everyone but the bride, who is too young to be served. "'You'll need something with more kick than that,' the bride's father said with heavy jocularity to his new son-in-law; the ritual jokes about the wedding night had a certain Panglossian character, since the bride was clearly several months pregnant. Another round of pink champagne, this time not on the house, and the bride began to cry. 'It was just as nice,' she sobbed, 'as I hoped and dreamed it would be'" (p. 83).

IV *West Of Eden*

John Gregory Dunne has noted that his wife "never writes about a place that is not hot. . . . The day she writes about a Boston winter will be the day it's all over" (see Davidson, p. 35). Accordingly, Didion's favorite vacation spot and the locus of much of her writing is our western-most state—the perpetually seasonable Islands of Hawaii.[10] However, there is something more involved in her Hawaiian essays than the author's preference for warm climates. In effect, she uses the islands as a perspective from which to examine various aspects of life on the mainland. She sees this exotic region as being an integral, if idiosyncratic, part of the larger American scene.

A case in point is her October 1976 *Esquire* essay on the Kahala Hilton—Hawaiian headquarters of the beautiful people. This essay is entitled—quite appropriately—"Where *Tonight Show* Guests Go to Rest" and it begins with a litany of familiar names. "The last time I visited the Kahala Hilton in Honolulu," Didion writes, "Rod Stewart was there, just off the road, and James Guercio was there, just off the road, and Helen Reddy was there, just off the road. Carol Burnett had recently come and gone, as had the queen of England. Totie Fields and Steve and Eydie Lawrence and Cher and Chastity Bono had also come and gone, but Joe Frazier was there, and the day he flew out Muhammad Ali arrived" (p. 25).

Clearly, this essay is meant to be a light, minor piece of journalism and its appearance in *Esquire* is not surprising. ("Where *Tonight Show* Guests Go to Rest" is the sort of inside look at celebrity life which appeals to people who eagerly await the next installment of Truman Capote's *Answered Prayers*.) And yet Didion is not writing a gossip column; she is trying instead to give us a generic sense of what life is like among a group of people who are widely recognized yet strangely insular in their ways:

They are personalities of a certain kind, these people who regard the Kahala as their private retreat. If they are not "just off the road," they are in "the hiatus," by which they mean the break in the filming of a television show. They are more often television people than motion-picture people. They are more apt to be mentioned in *People* than in *W*. Quite often they have just done two weeks at the Grand in Las Vegas, and more often than not they have also just "done Carson." (p. 26)

The Kahala is a place where the big news during a particular week is that the president of CBS has been deposed, or—as it is cryptically recounted among the initiated—that "Bob Wood is out." To have known or to have inferred this news a week or even a few days before it happened is considered a mark of status here at the Kahala. (It is probably to Didion's credit that she had to be told who Bob Wood was.) Perhaps the entertainment capitals of New York, Hollywood, and Las Vegas are less physical locations than they are floating metonymies. The "Tonight Show," like Hemingway's Paris, is apparently a moveable feast.

As interesting as her sketch about the Kahala may be, Didion's most definitive statement about Hawaii—and one of the finest essays she has written on any topic—is "Letter from Paradise, 21° 19′ N, 157° 52′ W" (*Slouching*, pp. 187–204). Here she uses personal reminiscence, historical and sociological commentary, and a few suggestive camera-eye descriptions to convey a sense of life on the islands. To understand this life, however, we must begin by sharing the author's childhood perception that Hawaii is, in fact, three places.

There was first the Hawaii of Pearl Harbor and of World War II. Then "when the war was over, there was another Hawaii, a big rock candy mountain in the Pacific which presented itself . . . in newspaper photographs of well-fed Lincoln-Mercury dealers relaxing beside an outrigger at the Royal Hawaiian Hotel" (p. 189). And finally, there is "a place which seemed to have to do neither with war nor with vacationing godmothers but only with the past, and with loss" (p. 189). This third Hawaii sees itself as a victim of Henry Kaiser, here pictured as a sort of mid-Pacific Snopes. Didion writes:

My aunt married into a family which had lived for generations in the Islands, but they did not even visit there any more; "Not since Mr. *Kaiser*," they would say, as if the construction of the Hawaiian Village Hotel on a few acres of reclaimed tidal flat near Fort De Russy had in one swing of the builder's crane wiped out their childhoods and their parents' childhoods, blighted forever some sub-tropical cherry orchard where every night in the soft blur of memory the table was set for forty-eight in case someone dropped by. (pp. 189–90)

Didion writes movingly about all three images of Hawaii, particularly about Hawaii as a graveyard for the casualties of war. Here her descriptions of the National Memorial Cemetery of the Pacific anticipate the searing evocation of that place in her account of the Vietnam burial in Punchbowl. Her focus in "Letter from Paradise . . . ," however, is primarily on memories of World War II. "They all seem to be twenty years old," she writes, "the boys buried up there in the crater of an extinct volcano named Punchbowl, twenty and nineteen and eighteen and sometimes not that old. 'SAMUEL FOSTER HARMON,' one stone reads. 'PENNSYLVANIA. PVT 27 REPL DRAFT 5 MARINE DIV. WORLD WAR II. APRIL 10 1928–MARCH 25 1945.' Samuel Foster Harmon died, at Iwo Jima, fifteen days short of his seventeenth birthday" (p. 193).

In a sense the Second World War helped bring Hawaii into the mainstream of American life. The paradise remembered so fondly by Didion's aunt's family was a regressive, feudal society actually destroyed more by war than by Henry Kaiser. And since relatively few Hawaiians benefited from this older society, it is understandable that *they* should view that society's end with a certain equanimity. (Of course, the aftermath of World War II brought similar dislocations, though on a smaller scale, to Didion's native California.) Hawaii, then, may be a highly isolated and atypical part of America, but as a part it is subject to some of the same social dynamics as the rest of the nation. Perhaps it can best be understood by an American of western origins who can say, "I sat as a child on California beaches and imagined that I saw Hawaii, a certain shimmer in the sunset, a barely perceptible irregularity glimpsed intermittently through squinted eyes" (p. 188).

"Letter from Paradise . . ." was written in 1966 when the social fabric of Hawaii was being shaped by the Vietnam war, when sailors in Honolulu got drunk "because they were no longer in Des Moines and not yet in Da Nang" ("Letter," p. 195). Eleven years later, however, with the Vietnam war over, Didion made a pilgrimage to the Islands to pay homage to a veteran of that earlier, global conflict, to the man who made Honolulu come alive in his novel *From Here to Eternity*—James Jones. Her account of that pilgrimage is contained in the final section of a long *White Album* sequence called "In the Islands."[11] Here she tells us something about Hawaii, about the role of place in fiction, and about the fleeting nature of artistic fame. She writes of Jones:

In June of 1977 he was dead and it was not possible to buy a copy of his great novel . . . in any of Honolulu's largest bookstores. "Is it a bestseller?" I was asked in one, and the golden child in charge of another suggested I try the psychic-science shelf. In that instant I thought I grieved for James Jones, a man I never met, but I think I grieved for all of us: for Jones, for myself, for the sufferers of mean guilts and for their exorcists, for Robert E. Lee Prewitt, for the Royal Hawaiian Hotel [12] and for this golden nitwit who believed eternity to be a psychic science. (p. 148)

Nevertheless, Jones's achievement is still remembered and revered by the soldiers at Schofield Barracks, the novelist's old army base and the setting of *From Here to Eternity*. An essential part of Didion's Honolulu pilgrimage is her drive to Schofield. "It had rained in the morning," she writes, "and the smell of eucalyptus was sharp in the air and I had again that familiar sense of having left the bright coast and entered a darker country. The black outline of the Waianae Range seemed obscurely oppressive. A foursome on the post golf course seemed to have been playing since 1940, and to be doomed to continue. A soldier in fatigues appeared to be trimming a bougain-villea hedge, swinging at it with a scythe, but his movements were hypnotically slowed, and the scythe never quite touched the hedge" (pp. 148–49). Arriving at Schofield, she visits the spots made famous by Jones and observes that while details may have changed, the army is still essentially as he had depicted it—"nothing more or less than life itself." "I wish I could tell you that on the day in May when James Jones died someone had played taps for him at Schofield Barracks," she concludes, "but I think this is not the way life goes" (p. 152).

This elegiac essay is a loving tribute to a man whom Didion knew only through a single remarkable novel. (Surely, one of the tasks of literary criticism is to evoke interest in the material being discussed, and this Didion does for James Jones and *From Here to Eternity*.) In the process, she tells us something simple, yet profound, about the nature of literature itself. She tells us that "certain places seem to exist mainly because someone has written about them. . . . A place belongs forever to whoever claims it hardest, remembers it most obsessively, wrenches it from itself, shapes it, renders it, loves it so radically that he remakes it in his image" (p. 146). As we shall see in the next chapter, one could reasonably maintain that Didion herself has laid just such imaginative claim to the remembered valleys of a California that has ceased to be.[13]

CHAPTER 7

The Real Eldorado

IN *How to Save Your Own Life* Erica Jong asserts that "California is a wet dream in the mind of New York."[1] And when one considers the image of the West in American literature, it is hard to argue with such an assertion. Indeed, our national psyche almost always has been burdened with an excess of adolescent optimism. Throughout the nineteenth century hordes of itinerant dreamers believed that a better life could be found, quite literally, over the next horizon. Such a fantasy, of course, was simply an extension of the European and early American belief in a New World Eden. As we are told in that passage from *Peck's 1837 New Guide to the West* which appears as an epigraph to *Run River*, "the real Eldorado is still further on."

Clearly, there was a paradox involved in our movement westward. The unsettled parts of the continent attracted those who found civilization to be decadent and corrupt. And yet, once settled, the West itself became part of that decadent and corrupt civilization. Our optimistic forebears, however, were slow to recognize this paradox. For them the settling of the frontier seemed an unmixed blessing. As Henry Nash Smith observes, "The Atlantic seaboard . . . represented the past, the shadow of Europe, cities, sophistication, a derivative and conventional life and literature. Beyond, occupying the overwhelming geographical mass of the continent, lay the West, a realm where nature loomed larger than civilization and where feudalism had never been established. There, evidently, would grow up the truly American society of the future."[2]

The appeal of that "virgin land" whose frontiers were constantly receding westward was neither simple nor unambiguous. To some the New World was an unspoiled garden, to be accepted and reverenced as it was found. To others it was a harrowing wilderness, inviting struggle and conquest. In a sense, though, as Leo Marx tells us,

America was *both* Eden and a howling desert; the actual conditions of life in the New World did lend plausibility to both images. The infinite resources of the virgin land really did make credible, in minds long habituated to the notion of unavoidable scarcity, the ancient dream of an abundant and harmonious life for all. Yet, at the same time, the savages, the limitless spaces, and the violent climate of the country did threaten to engulf the new civilization. . . . If America seemed to promise everything that men always had wanted, it also threatened to obliterate much of what they already had achieved.[3]

The situation which we face at the present time is, of course, radically different from that which confronted the early settlers. Although the hope of paradise was not realized, neither was the fear of annihilation. As a people we moved west and conquered the wilderness; but now the journey is over. Rather than leading to contentment and a sense of accomplishment, the end of the westward journey has infused in many people feelings of depression and betrayal. In John Steinbeck's "The Leader of the People," for example, we encounter an old man who once led a wagon train across the continent to California. Now he lives next to the ocean and spends most of his time telling bored listeners about his bygone adventures. His daughter says of the journey, "That was the big thing in my father's life. . . . It was a big thing to do, but it didn't last long enough."[4]

The old man in Steinbeck's story represents a kind of anachronistic heroism. In the modern world he has become a pathetic and laughable figure. He tells his grandson Jody, "There's a line of old men along the shore hating the ocean because it stopped them" (p. 119). While such rage is surely pointless, the grandfather is finally a sympathetic character. In a sense his spirit is both admirable and out of place in contemporary America. He is substantially correct when he tells Jody, "Westering has died out of the people. Westering isn't a hunger anymore. . . . It is finished" (p. 119).

The grandfather's despondency is perhaps endemic to the western experience. Although despair and frustration can be found in any region and in any age, there are valid psychological and historical reasons for the prevalence of such attitudes in recent California literature. Even if life is no worse in the West than elsewhere, our native American optimism tells us that the new Eden should be better than the old Gomorrah. And yet frequently it is not. For, as Jonas Spatz writes, "The westward movement, once symbolic of rebirth out of Old World privilege, oppression, and poverty, becomes a journey into despair. The American is betrayed not by the brutalities of the city but by the image of his own salvation."[5]

Needless to say, when we begin to talk of literature in terms of regional characteristics we must avoid the pitfalls of reductionism. It would be clearly wrong to think that all California novels are alike. (In fact, Walter Wells goes so far as to identify the indigenous characteristics of three distinct subregions in California literature: "the Olympian misanthropy or disinterestedness of Robinson Jeffers and Walter Van Tilburg Clark, the essential sanguinity and sentimentality of central valley writers like Saroyan and Steinbeck, and the sardonic and skeptical moralism of the more transient Hollywood-Southland writers.")[6] Yet, having duly noted the limitations of regionalism, one must still admit that a certain geographical area during a given historical period is sometimes the most appropriate setting for a particular kind of story. For this to be the case, however, more than just the quaint element of local color needs to be involved.

Since the most substantial instance of regional influence in contemporary writing is probably in the literature of the American South, it might help us to understand the effect of place on the creative imagination if we consider what makes that literature distinctively southern. In this regard an observation of Allen Tate's is particularly helpful. Tate suggests that prior to the First World War the characteristic mode of southern discourse was rhetorical, but that in recent years it has become dialectical; that is, the South has started to regard itself in an introspective and self-critical fashion. "The South not only reentered the world with the first World War; it looked around and saw for the first time since about 1830 that the Yankees were not to blame for everything."[7] (Indeed, it is frequently the case that an insular and traditional subculture which is in the process of being assimilated into the larger surrounding culture will produce a flowering of imaginative literature. Robert Penn Warren has suggested such a thesis as an explanation for the abundance of fine southern writers between the two world wars and of talented Jewish writers after World War II.[8])

It would seem, however, that California and the traditional South are as far removed from each other as any two regions possibly could be.[9] On the whole, California has not had nearly so traditional and insular a culture as that of the South. And yet, throughout much of American history, the image of California—as opposed to its reality—has had a fixed *mythic* identity. As the geographic limit of our movement westward, California represents a paradise yet to be regained. According to Didion, "it is characteristic of Californians to speak grandly of the past as if it had simultaneously begun, *tabula rasa*, and reached a happy ending on the day the wagons started west. . . . California is a place in which a boom mentality and a sense of Chekhovian loss meet in uneasy suspension; in which the mind is troubled by some buried but ineradicable suspicion that things had better work here, because here, beneath that immense bleached sky, is where we run out of continent" (*Slouching*, p. 172).

As we have seen in previous chapters, Didion's acute sense of her California heritage causes much of her journalism to be both regional and autobiographical in focus. ("In the middle of my life," she writes, "it occurs to me that I think differently because I come from the coast."[10]) Those writings which represent a fusion of her regional and autobiographical perspectives show how her geographical origins have affected Didion's sensibility; and conversely, the author's identity as a native daughter of the West helps her to illuminate the region in which she lives. We find this to be particularly true in her February 1976 *Esquire* column "Thinking About Western Thinking."

In that essay Didion contends that there is a certain psychology peculiar to western Americans. She writes: "It is 'different' to be Western, and to pretend that this is no longer or never was so is to ignore the narrative force of the story Westerners learn early: the story that the wilderness is redemptive, and that a radical break with civilization and its discontents is distinctly an option" (p. 14). She tells us that her own ancestors, women who came west by wagon, "were pragmatic and in their deepest instincts clinically radical, given to breaking clean with everything and everyone they knew" (p. 10). We also learn that the descendants of these women are a similarly restless lot. One of Didion's cousins is a librarian on Taiwan; another is a teacher on Guam; and the author's own mother "speaks of moving to the Australian outback." If Didion follows her own inclinations, however, she will eventually find herself in "Honiara, Guadalcanal, the Solomon Islands" (p. 10).

"Thinking About Western Thinking" ends on a whimsically confessional note, directing our attention to the present while suggesting possibilities for the future: "in the presence of certain high Eastern accents," Didion writes, "I fall so helplessly into the Okie diction of the Sacramento Valley as to be unintelligible. . . . A derisive barefoot populism creeps into my opinions at those very tables where I know it to be least acceptable. I find this refractory strain in myself neither useful nor attractive, but I do know where it comes from. I also know this: I have on my passport an unused current visa for the Solomon Islands. So does my husband. So does our daughter" (p. 14).

I *Fire and Rain*

In *Bright Book of Life* Alfred Kazin points out that Didion "describes southern California in terms of fire, rattlesnakes, cave-ins, earthquakes . . . , and the terrible wind called the Santa Ana" (p. 191). This elemental understanding of place, it seems to me, is best illustrated in the essays "Los Angeles Notebook" (*Slouching*, pp. 217–24), "Quiet Days in Malibu" (*Album*, pp. 209–23), and "Holy Water" (*Album*, pp. 59–66).

In the first of these its author describes the sense of foreboding which Southern Californians feel prior to the onslaught of a Santa Ana wind: "The baby frets. The maid sulks. I rekindle a waning argument with the telephone company, then cut my losses and lie down, given over to whatever is in the air. To live with the Santa Ana is to accept, consciously or unconsciously, a deeply mechanistic view of human behavior" (p. 217). And a bit later she writes:

The city burning is Los Angeles's deepest image of itself: Nathanael West perceived that, in *The Day of the Locust*; and at the time of the 1965 Watts riots what struck the imagination most indelibly were the fires. For days one could drive the Harbor Freeway and see the city on fire, just as we had always known it would be in the end. Los Angeles weather is the weather of catastrophe, of apocalypse. . . . The violence and unpredictability of the Santa Ana affect the entire quality of life in Los Angeles, accentuate its impermanenence, its unreliability. The wind shows us how close to the edge we are. (pp. 220–21)

The extreme aridity of Los Angeles during that time of year known as "the fire season," coupled with the fierceness of the Santa Ana wind, makes brush fires a not uncommon occurrence there. In 1978, for example, a brush fire caught in Agoura, in the San Fernando Valley, and quickly spread across 25,000 acres and thirteen miles to the coast. There it jumped the Pacific Coast Highway—principal residential street of Malibu—and became "a half-mile fire storm generating winds of 100 miles per hour and temperatures up to 2500 degrees Fahrenheit" ("Quiet Days," p. 223). "Refugees huddled on Zuma Beach," Didion writes. "Horses caught fire and were shot on the beach, birds exploded in the air. Houses did not explode but imploded, as in a nuclear strike" (p. 223).

The fire destroyed 197 houses, many of which belonged to or had belonged to people Didion knew. She tells of visiting a local orchid grower—Amado Vazquez—and finding his greenhouse in ruins: "The place was now a range not of orchids but of shattered glass and melted metal and the imploded shards of . . . thousands of chemical beakers" (p. 223). After bidding Amado Vazquez good-bye, she goes with her husband and daughter "to look at the house on the Pacific Coast Highway in which we had lived for seven years. The fire had come to within 125 feet of the property, then stopped or turned or been beaten back, it was hard to tell which" (p. 223). In any case, since the Dunnes had recently moved back into town from Malibu, the house was no longer theirs.

According to Bernard DeVoto, "the West begins where the average annual rainfall drops below twenty inches." To Joan Didion's mind, "this is maybe the best definition of the West I have ever read" ("Water," p. 65). In meditating on the significance of water for the region in which she lives, Didion gives us a very different picture of California from that of the city burning. The controlling element here is essentially life-giving and the tone of her prose is more lyrical than apocalyptic.

Appropriately, the essay begins on a nostalgic note as its author remembers a morning when she was "seventeen years old and caught, in a military surplus life raft, in the construction of the Nimbus Afterbay Dam on the American River near Sacramento" (p. 60). She recalls trying to open a tin of anchovies with capers when the raft began to spin "into the narrow chute through which the river had been temporarily diverted." She also recalls "being deliriously happy" (p. 60).

The specific occasion for this essay is Didion's trip to the Operation Control Center of the California State Water Project. The project's main undertaking on the day of her visit is the draining of Quail, a Los Angeles County reservoir which contains a capacity of 1,636,018,000 gallons. "I knew at that moment," she writes, "that I had missed the only vocation for which I had any instinctive affinity: I wanted to drain Quail myself" (p. 62).

Later she tells of a poem by Karl Shapiro which she had torn from a magazine and pinned to her kitchen wall. Although the fragment of paper is now on the wall of a sixth kitchen and crumbles whenever she touches it, the last stanza of the poem has, for Didion, "the power of a prayer:

> *It is raining in California, a straight rain*
> *Cleaning the heavy oranges on the bough*
> *Filling the gardens till the gardens flow*
> *Shining the olives, tiling the gleaming tile,*
> *Waxing the dark camellia leaves more green*
> *Flooding the daylong valleys like the Nile."* (p. 65)

"I had no further business in this room," she concludes, "and yet I wanted to stay the day. I wanted to be the one, that day, who was shining the olives, filling the gardens and flooding the daylong valleys like the Nile. I want it still" (p. 66).

Didion's writings about modern California, like those of Nathanael West, have often been characterized as portraits of a wasteland. (Certainly the image of Los Angeles burning bears some symbolic affinity to the Unreal City of Eliot and Baudelaire.) However, the flowing of water carries with it the possibility of growth and fertility. (It can also symbolize power and frequently be the focus of a struggle for power. One thinks, in this regard, of the respective images of water and drought in Roman Polanski's *Chinatown*.) Moreover, water can be both a cleansing and a purging element. Indeed, we need only turn to a passage from her essay "On Morality" to see that for Joan Didion it is so. "Were I to follow my conscience," she writes, "it would lead me out onto the desert with Marion Faye, out to where he stood in *The Deer Park* looking east to Los Alamos and praying, as if for rain, that it would happen *". . . let it come and clear the rot and the stench and the stink, let it come for all of everywhere, just so it comes and the world stands clear in the white dead dawn" (Slouching,* p. 161).[11]

II *Goldengroves Unleaving*

Didion is never so lyrical about the California of her youth as to lose sight of its shortcomings, nor is she ever so pessimistic about our present condition as to indulge a sentimental nihilism. (A sense of boundless hope or one of total defeat is rarely enlightening or particularly interesting, while an "uneasy suspension" between the two can be both.) The pervasive tone of Didion's prose is one of irony. And it is an irony molded by the exigencies of place. If California is the place where a *tabula rasa* mentality merges with a Chekhovian sense of loss, then western experience is by its very nature paradoxical. In Steinbeck's image of "a line of old men . . . hating the ocean because it stopped them" we see the absurd culmination of an age-long search for the earthly paradise.[12] In California we have come to the end of the yellow brick road.

This sense of an ending, this contrast of past hope and present disillusionment, is perhaps the dominant theme in Didion's writings about the West. As Kazin says of her, "the story between the lines of *Slouching Towards Bethlehem* is surely not so much 'California' as it is her ability to make us share her passionate sense of it" (*Bright Book,* p. 190). In a way Didion is to the upper middle class of the

Central Valley what Faulkner was to the Sartorises and Snopeses of Mississippi—a chronicler of social change and fragmentation.[13] And nowhere is this change and fragmentation more movingly discussed than in the essay "Notes from a Native Daughter" (*Slouching*, pp. 171–86).

In this essay Didion makes several tongue-in-cheek comparisons between her native region and the Holy Land. For example, we twice encounter the following tourist-guide parody:

Q. *In what way does the Holy Land resemble the Sacramento Valley?*
A. *In the type and diversity of its agricultural products.* (pp. 174, 181)[14]

Elsewhere she writes: "In at least one respect California . . . resembles Eden: it is assumed that those who absent themselves from its blessings have been banished, exiled by some perversity of heart. Did not the Donner-Reed Party, after all, eat its own dead to reach Sacramento?" (p. 176). Perhaps she is attempting through the sardonic tone of such passages to avoid idealizing the pre-Sunbelt West. Indeed, far from harboring illusions about the way things were, she tells us quite frankly that "this has been a story not about Sacramento at all, but about the things we lose and the promises we break as we grow older" (p. 186). It is through such honest introspection that Didion maintains a balanced perspective. Once again, the focus of her writing is both regional and autobiographical. And its mood, ultimately neither satiric nor maudlin, is genuinely elegiac.

She tells us that "going back to California is not like going back to Vermont, or Chicago; Vermont and Chicago are relative constants, against which one measures one's own change. All that is constant about the California of my childhood is the rate at which it disappears" (p. 176). To illustrate this sad truth Didion recalls a scene which is decidedly non-Edenic, but which is part of a vanished past. On Saint Patrick's Day 1948 she saw the state legislature in action. It was "a dismal experience; a handful of florid assemblymen, wearing green hats, were reading Pat-and-Mike jokes into the record" (p. 176). Now when she thinks of the legislators she sees them still in green hats "or sitting around on the veranda of the Senator Hotel fanning themselves and being entertained" by emissaries of Artie Samish—a legendary lobbyist who once said, "Earl Warren may be the governor of the state, but I'm the governor of the legislature" (pp. 176–77).

Although the author remembers these scenes with obvious affection, she does not try to gainsay their tawdriness. She simply juxtaposes a vision of the past with one of the present and allows us to draw our own conclusions. She tells us, for example, that "there is no longer a veranda at the Senator Hotel—it was turned into an airline ticket office . . . , and in any case the legislature has largely deserted the Senator for the flashy motels north of town, where the tiki torches flame and the steam rises off the heated pools in the cold Valley night" (p. 177).

In "Notes from a Native Daughter" the final scene is one of those rare vignettes which sum up the experience of a region, while simultaneously addressing itself to the larger human condition. Joan Didion calls it "a Sacramento story." According to this story a rancher once lived outside of town on a spread of six or seven thousand acres. His one daughter went abroad and married a title and brought that title home to live on the ranch. Her father then built them a large house, consisting of music rooms, conservatories, and a ballroom. "They needed a ballroom because they entertained: people from abroad, people from San Francisco, house parties that lasted weeks and involved special trains" (p. 185). These people are now long dead; but an old man, the only son of the rancher's daughter and of her title, still lives on the place. He does not live in the house for over the years the house has burned, room by room and wing by wing. Now "only the chimneys of the great house are still standing, and its heir lives in their shadow, lives by himself on the charred site, in a house trailer" (p. 185).

Didion then reflects: "That is a story my generation knows; I doubt that the next will know it, the children of the aerospace engineers. Who would tell it to them? Their grandmothers live in Scarsdale, and they have never met a great aunt. . . . They will have lost the real past and gained a manufactured one, and there will be no way for them to know, no way at all, why a house trailer should stand alone on seven thousand acres outside town" (pp. 185, 186).

Although "Notes from a Native Daughter" was first published in 1965, the sense of loss which this essay conveys can be found in Didion's writing as far back as her college days at Berkeley. Consider, for example, her story "Sunset." Published in the student literary magazine *Occident* (Spring 1956), this story tells of a young woman who—like Thomas Wolfe's George Webber—experiences the difficulty of trying to return to a home which no longer exists. A remarkably accomplished story for a writer so young, "Sunset" serves as an excellent introduction to its author's later fiction, particularly to her novel *Run River*.

The focal character of Didion's story is Laura Cavanaugh Gannon, a native Californian who—after her father's death—had moved to New York with her mother. Laura is now married to Charlie Gannon, a well-meaning but insensitive businessman from Chicago who is considerably older than she. As the story opens Charlie and Laura are driving to the graveyard where her father is buried. (Although the location is never specified, Didion's descriptions leave little doubt that her setting is the Sacramento Valley.)[15] Laura is clearly disturbed by the changes which have taken place since last she was home:

Nothing was the same after twelve years; she could not go back. All the land had been sold and subdivided (by dreaming men like Charlie, men with their eyes on the main chance), and even the house in which she had lived her first sixteen years and been turned into a day nursery—Barbara Murray (but her name was St. John, now) sent her children there, and had said that they were using Laura's wildflower and organdy bedroom as a finger-painting gallery. She could visit Barbara and the others now and they could talk of the same things, but there was always the barrier, strong as steel, of time and other worlds. (p. 21)

Among those other worlds is the one to which Charlie Gannon belongs. Although he lives in Chicago and travels to the Coast only on business, he is the prototype of the New West carpetbagger—a figure more fully realized in *Run River*'s Ryder Channing. (As they are driving to the graveyard Laura reflects that "if Charlie were developing this land he would promote it as suburban upper-middle potential, and restrict it. 'In the California Manner,' he would say. 'Casual Country Living.' And he would call it 'River Oaks,' and keep the promotion subdued" [p. 23].) Charlie, then, functions in this story as something of a sociological symbol—and, unfortunately, as little else. A weakly drawn figure, he possesses neither the charm nor the menace of Didion's later, more vital male characters.

Although we do not know the source of Laura's original attraction to Charlie, his age may well have been a salient consideration. Since she had had a very close relationship with her father (and a very strained one with her mother), it could be that in Charlie she hopes to find a substitute father. This desire, however, creates intolerable contradictions when Charlie accompanies Laura on the pilgrimage to her actual father's grave. Indeed, when her husband attempts to console her by asking what more he can do for her, Laura lashes out: "Perhaps you should have married my mother" (p. 27). (In a sense Laura probably wishes that she *could* trade husbands with her mother. Although no overtly incestuous feelings are suggested here, it is clear that Laura's bond with her father was stronger than any she will ever forge with Charlie.) If it is the memory of her father which accounts in large part for Laura's sense of identity with her childhood home, his death may help to explain her present alienation from that home.[16] And her marriage to Charlie—the inadequate substitute father from the East—is simply the most immediate reminder of that alienation.

At one point she tries vainly to tell Charlie what it is she has lost. "It was always lovely on the river," she says. "Everything hung in a kind of fluid suspension. No time ever" (p. 26). When her husband insists that "you can't just want suspension," Laura replies, "It's all that counts" (p. 26); and when he says in desperation, "Everything can belong to us," she responds epigrammatically, "Everything can belong to us. . . . But we don't belong to anything" (p. 26). It is a plaintive lament and one that is echoed throughout Didion's writings about modern California.

III *Kingdom of the Mad*[17]

Joan Didion's first novel—*Run River*—tells of the twenty-year marriage of Everett and Lily Knight McClellan. Both children of prosperous Sacramento Valley ranchers, Everett and Lily begin their life together by eloping to Reno. However, shortly after their wedding and the subsequent birth of their two children, the couple is separated as Everett goes away to the Second World War. Feeling lonely and betrayed, Lily has an affair with a neighboring rancher and conceives his child. When Everett comes home from the war, having been given a hardship discharge due to the death of his father, he is unable to cope with his wife's confessions of infidelity. Lily then slips away to San Francisco to have an abortion. And in the ensuing years she and Everett increasingly live lives of mutual recrimination.

As the McClellans' marriage continues to disintegrate, the novel's focus widens to include the relationship of Everett's sister Martha with a charming young social climber named Ryder Channing. After five years of enjoying steady company and frequent sexual intimacies with Martha, Ryder abruptly marries a young socialite—Miss Bugsy Dupree. Unable to put her life back together, Martha takes a boat out one stormy night and drowns. At Everett's insistence she is buried on the ranch.

As the years go by Everett and Lily grow further apart and Lily, herself, finally takes up with Ryder Channing. When the novel opens Ryder, who has been awaiting an assignation with Lily on the levee of the McClellan ranch, is shot by Everett. We are then afforded a retrospective view of the preceding two decades, 1938–1959. When we return to time present, Everett and Lily are anticipating the arrival of the sheriff. Lily remains in the house as Everett returns to the murder scene. A second shot is heard and we, along with Lily, realize that Everett McClellan has taken his own life. The beginning and end of Didion's novel have the makings of tabloid melodrama ("IRATE HUSBAND SHOOTS RIVAL, SELF"). However, in the intervening chapters, we have seen a picture of personal and cultural disintegration of sufficient power to raise melodrama to the level of serious art.

The story of *Run River* is told from what is technically a third-person-omniscient point of view. The narrator's focus, however, is confined to three characters: to Lily and Martha primarily, and on occasion to Everett. (We overhear Everett's thoughts, for example, concerning Lily's attire for her tryst with Ryder Channing: *"'Jesus Christ,'* he thought with abstract tenderness, *'high-heeled shoes to get screwed on the beach'"* [p. 15].)[18] Didion's narrator does not intrude with moral pronouncements or with personal digressions in the manner of Henry Fielding or George Eliot; nor does she summarize the future lives of her characters as does Charles Dickens. Hers is a rigidly self-limited omniscience.[19] By avoiding first-person narration, Didion is able to speak in a voice not unlike her own. And by eschewing limited narration, even of the third-person variety, she manages to give considerable stress to the experiences of *both* Martha and Lily.

Even the most cursory reflection indicates that *Run River*, told from a different point of view, would have been much narrower in scope than the novel which Didion actually wrote. To begin with, no single character has access to more than part of the novel's story. Martha dies a decade before the final confrontation between her brother and Ryder Channing; Lily, who is present for most of the novel's action, is not close enough to her sister-in-law to tell Martha's story with proper sympathy and insight; and Everett does not know himself or others well enough to make narrative order out of the chaos of all their lives. (True, Didion could have achieved an ironic effect by using an unreliable narrator; however, she seems to prefer straightforward exposition to arcane technical experiments.) Still, the narrative voice which Didion does employ is not simply the lone option to survive a process of elimination; instead, as a functional element of the novel, it serves specific tonal and thematic purposes. Consider, for example, the narrator's discussion of Lily's past suitors. We learn of two of the young men whom Lily dated during her year at Berkeley. In describing the first of these, the narrator sounds very much like an urbane prose stylist named Joan Didion:

Out with a Sigma Chi who had just been accepted at Princeton Theological Seminary . . . , [Lily] had attempted some banter about Reinhold Niebuhr; when that failed, she admired the way he played the ukelele. After several drinks, he told her a couple of *double entendre* stories, and although she neither understood them nor thought he should be telling them to her, she laughed appreciatively. When he asked her if she would like to drive up in the Berkeley Hills, she smiled with delight and said it sounded like fun; later, she reflected that it had not been entirely his fault that he had misinterpreted her behavior that evening, which had ended in front of an all-night drugstore on Shattuck Avenue where, the prospective theologian told Lily, he could get some rubbers. ("Rubbers?" she had said, and he had looked at her. "Safes. Contraceptives." She had begun shaking her head then, unable to think what to say, and he, sobered, had driven her in silence up the hill to the Pi Phi house.) (pp. 51-52)

Lily's second admirer at Berkeley is a Jewish graduate student from New York named Leonard Sachs.[20] He and Lily eat dinner by candlelight in his apartment and she listens to him expound on left-wing social issues. When he notices her knitting a sweater for her father, Leonard urges Lily to "utilize what slender talents she had by teaching handicrafts in a settlement house. Unable to locate 'settlement houses' in the Berkeley Yellow pages, she finally abandoned that project" (p. 52). She even invites him to the ranch for a day during spring vacation and he arrives conspicuously carrying a copy of Steinbeck's *In Dubious Battle*. Lily refers to Leonard Sachs as her "haunted lover": "although," the narrator tells us, "he was, literally, neither" (p. 53). I suspect, though, that in thinking of him as such Lily reveals something about her own needs and sensibility. Part of her wants a "haunted lover," and much later in her life Ryder Channing assumes that very role.

These flashbacks to Lily's years at Berkeley, however, do not represent the most evident manipulation of time in the novel. Indeed, about 85 percent of *Run River* consists of flashbacks. In the first thirty pages of the novel we learn of Lily's affair with Ryder Channing, of Channing's death at Everett's hands, and of Martha's drowning. About the only thing that is not revealed at the outset is Everett's suicide. We therefore approach the bulk of the novel with a sense of fatalism that is vaguely reminiscent of conventional American naturalism. Yet Didion is too much of a moralist to let her characters totally off the hook. Even if these characters cannot control the circumstances of their lives, they can at least try to act well in the face of adversity. Lily's final wish for Everett is that he had been a good man.

At one level what we have in *Run River* is the story of a traditional, agrarian culture which is being destroyed by the solipsistic values of the postwar boom. Since much southern literature is also concerned with the disappearance of an old order, *Run River* is in a limited way thematically akin to that literature.[21] Certainly we can see some rough similarities between the Mississippi of 1866 and the California of 1946. In each case the end of a war has brought the end of an era. While the reconstruction of the South was accomplished by carpet-baggers who employed violence and fraud, the social landscape of California was just as radically transformed by the more insidious influence of real-estate speculators and aerospace engineers. It is ironic, therefore, that Ryder Channing—the character who most exemplifies the New West—is himself a native of Tennessee.

Long before Channing arrives on the scene, however, the old order begins to break up. The first sign of this break-up occurs when Lily's father—Walter Knight—loses the 1938 California gubernatorial election to an Okie populist named Hank Catlin. Walter tells Lily, "We're in the era of the medicine man. We're going to have snake oil every Thursday. Dr. Townsend is going to administer it personally, with an unwilling assist from Sheridan Downey" (pp. 44–45). A bit later he says, "Different world, Lily. Different rules. But we'll beat them at their own game. . . . Because you've got in your little finger more brains and more guts than all those Okies got put together" (p. 45).

Just after Walter Knight's death Lily remembers a childhood trip with her father to the family graveyard. There she traced out the names on the gravestones until she came to the oldest grave: "*Matthew Broderick Knight, January 2, 1847, until December 6, 1848.*" The child, according to an old family story, had been born in Kentucky and had begun to burn with infant fever on the way west. Another child in the party had died of that same fever, but his mother had carried his body in her arms for three days, telling no one, afraid that they would bury her baby before coming to a station.[22] Matthew Knight, however, lived out the crossing; "he died instead in a room in Sacramento that first winter, while his father, Lily's great-great grandfather, was building the first house on the ranch" (p. 84).

The child's mother, "twenty years old that winter, was deranged for months, believing herself at home in Bourbon County even as she hauled buckets of Sacramento River silt to cover the hardpan around her raw house" (p. 84). During her illness she had wanted to grow a garden of forget-me-nots and love-lies-bleeding and the dogwood she remembered from her mother's kitchen stoop. (She had even ordered that her child's gravestone bear the inscription: *"By the rivers of Babylon, there we sat down."*) But as the summer broke, she began to feel better and eventually "planted those same alien poppies and lupines that grew on the child's grave." Indeed, "the symbolic nature of Amanda Broderick Knight's first garden on the ranch was, for the Knights, the story's *raison d'etre*. 'I think nobody owns land,'" Walter Knight had said to Lily, 'until their dead are in it'" (p. 84).

Didion, however, is careful not to paint too idyllic a picture of the conservative western rancher. Everett's father, John McClellan, for example, is an irascible reactionary whose comments on various topics provide the novel with some of its few moments of humor. At one point he says to Lily, "Here's one fact you won't learn in college, Miss Lily Knight: there's nobody in God's green world has less native intelligence than a goddamn wetback." We learn, too, that

Everett had once explained that his father referred to all Mexicans and to most South Americans—including the President of Brazil, who had once been entertained on the river—as goddamn wetbacks, and to all Orientals as goddamn Filipinos. . . . Easterners fell into two camps: goddamn pansies and goddamn Jews. On the whole, both categories had to do with attitudes, not facts, and occasionally they overlapped. His daughter Sarah had for example married a goddamn pansy and gone East to live, where she picked up those goddamn Jew ideas. (pp. 56–57)

While Everett is away during the war Lily and her father-in-law play hearts for pennies, or for toothpicks when no pennies are available. On one of the rare occasions when Lily wins, she makes the mistake of losing her toothpicks. Although she is willing to forego the 33 cents to which the toothpicks would have entitled her, John McClellan holds up dinner for an hour and fifteen minutes while he, Lily, and China Mary—Didion's west-coast equivalent of the southern mammy—search for the missing toothpicks. Later that evening McClellan lectures Lily all through dinner on *"the importance of property rights and keeping one's accounts in order. It was, he said, the American way"* (p. 110).[23]

In a sense John McClellan is the last of a breed. Although he may not be as socially enlightened as his son Everett, he is more sensitive to the nuances of tradition. It had been a custom of John McClellan's, for example, to invite the foreman and his wife to the house on the

night the hop picking was finished. However, his son's foreman—
Henry Sears—departs for town on that festive night before Everett
can speak to him, "even if Everett had intended speaking to him"
(p. 149). Nor does Everett know what he could have said to Sears had
he invited him. People had always responded to Everett's father. "He
would have known, as Everett did not know, how to talk to Henry
Sears" (p. 150). Uncomfortable with the amenities of the past and
unwilling to accept the anomie of the future, Everett—like the
speaker in Matthew Arnold's "Stanzas from the Grande Char-
treuse"—is caught between two worlds: one dead, the other powerless
to be born.

But at least Everett remains on the land. His sister Sarah leaves for
the East, perhaps "exiled by some perversity of heart." And new
arrivals like Ryder Channing do not even know of the abandoned
valley traditions.[24] We get a revealing glimpse of Channing's attitude
toward his new home in a conversation which he has with Everett and
Martha. "The point is we need everything out here," Ryder says.
"Absolutely *tabula rasa*. Christ, within the next ten, fifteen years
somebody could make a fortune in the *agency* business" (p. 158).[25]
(When Everett—who resents Channing's use of the first-person
plural—reflects on his own view of advertising, he sees it as another
world, one "teeming with immigrants and women who spend the day
in art galleries and elevator operators who called you by name if you
were a crack *Life* photographer" [p. 159].) Ryder finally gets a chance
to test his theories when—shortly after his marriage to Bugsy
Dupree—he is placed in charge of a suburban housing development
called Riverside City. In response to a prospective Riverside City
couple from Chicago who inquire about the appearance of a plastic
lining then being installed in the bottom of Riverside Lake, Channing
writes: "*You can relax. The lining will be covered with six inches of
earth, so unless you come out to inspect it now, you'll never see it*"
(p. 210).

Ultimately, Ryder Channing is a disturbing and enigmatic character. Had Didion made him more offensive than she did, his appeal to
Martha and later to Lily would not have been credible. And yet, she
could not make him an altogether noble rogue and still have him do
the damage that he does. In trying to pursue a middle course, Didion
fails to make Channing as convincing as he needs to be in order to
bear the weight that he carries in the novel. Still, there is nothing
vague or unreal about Martha or Lily. And one's sense of their reality
is not fatally damaged by an inability to believe fully in Ryder
Channing.

In many ways the strongest and most tragic character in *Run River* is Martha McClellan. Lily is too confused, too passive, to elicit our respect. (One is reminded of what Norman Mailer says about Saul Bellow's *Seize the Day*: "It is not demanding to write about characters considerably more defeated than oneself."[26]) Martha, on the other hand, possesses wit, charm, and character; everything but the ability to survive.[27] Indeed, Martha's tragedy is what Joan Didion might call a Central Valley story. (I suspect that Lily's neuroses are rooted in the character of our time and are not dependent on a particular setting.) Martha's very reality is defined by her sense of belonging to a place and to a tradition. It is only fitting that her destruction be due at least in part to the rapacity of a carpetbagger and that she be buried on the ranch. For she belongs to that ranch as much as its fields and its crops do, as much as its deadly river does. She alone of the younger generation would have known how to talk to Henry Sears (p. 150).

Martha's deeply rooted sense of tradition is apparent when she and Lily see Everett off at the train depot prior to his departure for the army. Here, Martha gives her brother a gift: *"The McClellan Journal: An Account of an Overland Journey to California in the Year 1848."* And Lily reflects:

Everett and Martha. . . . Forward into battle with the Cross before. She remembered her surprise at finding on the walls of Martha's room, when they had been children and she had been sent to play at the McClellan place, neither Degas ballet dancers nor scenes from *Alice in Wonderland* but a framed deed signed by John Sutter in 1847, a matted list of the provisions carried on an obscure crossing in 1852, a detailed relief map of the Humboldt Sink, and a large lithograph of Donner Pass on which Martha had printed, in two neat columns, the names of the casualties and the survivors of the Donner-Reed crossing. (pp. 99–100)

Although Martha's sense of regional heritage remains with her to the end, the events which immediately precede her death and those which occur on the morning after powerfully suggest the breakdown of both her romantic and familial ties. To begin with, on the afternoon of her death Martha is paid a visit by Ryder Channing. Feeling that despite his marriage he should be able to enjoy Martha's favors at will, Channing assaults her: "'You want it,' he said. She had her legs crossed and her face turned away from him. . . . 'What difference do you think it makes now,' [he continues.] He pushed her skirt up around her waist. 'After I've screwed you maybe four, five times a week every week for the past five years'" (p. 215).

After Ryder leaves, Martha lies in bed until Lily and the children return home. They are going to the Saint Patrick's Day parade in town and they invite Martha to go with them.[28] She imagines what the parade will be like:

"You know what it'll be. There'll be a bagpipe band playing 'The Campbells are Coming.' The Air Force Band playing 'Loch Lomand.' And a battalion of small girls in spangled two-piece bathing suits and white plastic Stetsons doing close-order drill to 'Temptation.' *You-came-Ah was a-lone-Ah Should-a-known— You were Taymp-tay-shun.* . . . 'Temptation' will be *sung*—through a public address system on a truck behind the small girls—by a mother wearing a rose crepe dress with bugle beads, a short red car coat, and harlequin-framed glasses. . . . There will also be the Sheriff's Posse: fifteen dentists on fifteen palominos." (pp. 216–17)

Later at the parade Martha retreats to the Rexall drugstore. When she returns, "rain streamed down her face, across her sunglasses, down the neck of her unbuttoned raincoat" (p. 218). She had been trying to call her expatriated sister Sarah in Philadelphia, to tell her about the parade. After some confusion concerning the time difference between Sacramento and Philadelphia, Martha says to Lily: "If it's midnight there, as you insist it is, it's too late. . . . I didn't want to go home and I thought I might go there, but it's too late" (p. 219). As the chapter ends Lily maintains, "I don't know what you're *talk*ing about." *"Sarah. I'm talking about my sister,"* Martha replies. *"I wanted to talk to Sarah. If you don't mind"* (p. 219).

"They buried Martha's body beneath the cherry tree near the levee on the morning of the twenty-second of March" (p. 220).[29] Thus, as the next chapter opens, we learn of Martha's fate. She had taken a boat out on the flooding river and when her body was recovered it was too late to save her life. Everett stands at his sister's graveside and repeats the prayer that he and Martha had learned as children: *"Gentle Jesus, meek and mild. . . . Look upon a little child. Pity her simplicity and suffer her to come to thee"* (p. 223). This painful ritual is strangely moving, perhaps because it is so out of place. People no longer bury the dead on their own land. (In fact, Everett is defying a law pushed through the legislature by the undertaker's lobby.) And Martha is no longer simple or a child. With her passing we see the passing of the old order. People responded to her, as people once had responded to her father, each in his own way. Her niece Julie cries, "My Martha, my Martha." And Ryder Channing, so full of himself, at first believes the news of her death to be a hoax.

Although Martha's drowning has an impact on all of Didion's

major characters, Everett is the one most deeply affected. His relationship with his sister had been unusually close, as he and Martha seemed to reinforce each other's sense of identity. (In the scene at the railroad depot, for example, we see that the bond between Everett and Martha is such that even Lily becomes an outsider.) While it would be reading too much into the novel to infer an incestuous relationship, there is clearly a kind of *psychic* marriage between brother and sister. ("'You might marry Everett,' Martha McClellan had suggested to Lily, once when they were both children, 'if I decide not to'" [p. 48].) Indeed, I suspect that Everett's murder of Ryder Channing is caused less by Channing's affair with Lily than by his previous behavior toward Martha. (Everett's cuckoldry may give him an excuse for killing Ryder, but we must remember that others in the valley have bedded Lily with impunity.) Although an essentially benign figure, Everett responds violently to an accumulation of wrongs and—in the process—accomplishes his own destruction.

With Martha gone from the novel, the focus of *Run River* is directed increasingly toward Lily—a profoundly alienated woman. What is not clear, however, is the precise cause of Lily's alienation. Why should she, possessing basically the same heritage as Everett and Martha, be an outsider in her own community? The answer, I suspect, has something to do with the death of Walter Knight. The sort of spiritual symbiosis which Walter and Lily enjoy is similar to that which exists elsewhere in the novel between Martha and Everett and in "Sunset" between Laura and Mr. Cavanaugh. (When Lily finds out that Walter has drowned, she says, *"I'm not myself if my father's dead"* [p. 78].) Surely it is no accident that Lily's memory of her visit to the family graveyard—a sort of last-gasp recollection of her frontier heritage—is most intense just after Walter's death. Her sense of rootedness is defined largely in terms of her relationship to her father. When he is gone, so too is Lily's link with the past.[30]

Nor are her links with the future any less tenuous. Even the opportunity for maternal love proves elusive. The last scene in which we see her with one of her children makes Lily's plight painfully evident: "After Julie had gone to sleep Lily sat down in the dark by her bed. She wanted to hold Julie's hand, flung out from the striped lavender and white sheets, but was afraid that she would wake her. Instead she sat with her hands in her lap listening to Julie's even breathing, and when Julie woke and looked at her with the tears beginning in her eyes again, Lily only smoothed her hair. 'Go to sleep baby,' she said, unable to explain to Julie, any more than she could explain to herself, just where the trouble had begun" (pp. 253–54).[31]

When the highway patrol arrives to investigate the carnage on the dock, Lily brushes the leaves from the arm that she had held around Everett. And she begins to "wonder what she would say . . . to Knight and to Julie" (p. 264).

At times the individual reality which we encounter in this novel is so immediate that we are apt to lose sight of *Run River*'s larger historic and regional implications. And yet, those implications are pervasive. Although Joan Didion has not written a novel which is— in a narrow and provincial sense—*about* California, that novel is a regional tragedy in the same way that the writings of William Faulkner and Tennessee Williams are regional tragedies. For if California is the place where a geographical eschatology leads to a sense of disillusionment and loss, then the social fragmentation depicted in *Run River* is appropriate to a California setting. As if to emphasize this point, Didion includes some observations on the journey west at the very climax of her novel. Here Lily, sitting in her needlepoint chair, virtually anticipating Everett's suicide, thinks back over her life and remembers the lives of her ancestors. And she wonders:

What had it all been about: all the manqué promises, the failures of love and faith and honor; Martha buried out there by the levee in a $250 dress from Magnin's with river silt in the seams . . . ; [Lily's own] mother sitting alone this afternoon in the big house upriver writing out invitations for the Admission Day Fiesta and watching *Dick Clark's American Bandstand* because the Dodgers were rained out; Everett down there on the dock with his father's .38. She, her mother, Everett, Martha, the whole family gallery: they carried the same blood, come down through twelve generations of circuit riders, county sheriffs, Indian fighters, country lawyers, Bible readers, one obscure United States Senator from a frontier state a long time ago; two hundred years of clearings in Virginia and Kentucky and Tennessee and then the break, the void into which they gave their rosewood chests, their silver brushes; the cutting clean which was to have redeemed them all. They had been a particular kind of people, their particular virtues called up by a particular situation, their particular flaws waiting there through all those years, unperceived, unsuspected, glimpsed only cloudily by one or two in each generation, by a wife whose bewildered eyes wanted to look not upon Eldorado but upon her mother's dogwood. . . . What is it you want, she had asked Everett tonight. It was a question she might have asked them all. (pp. 262–63)

Finally, it is necessary to determine whether *Run River* stresses thematic scope at the expense of structural coherence. Would this novel have been a more unified work of art had Didion focused only on one of her principal female characters, or is there an important connection which makes Lily's story and Martha's part of a larger aesthetic unity? I would argue that such a unity exists and that it must be understood in terms of the contrast between Lily and Martha. If Martha is a sort of tragic heroine, clearly Lily is not. And since *Run River* concentrates more on Lily than on Martha, one must conclude that Didion does not find tragedy to be a representative mode of experience for our time. In the juxtaposition of the respective destinies of these two women there is an implied bathos. While Martha has found an uneasy rest, Lily must drag herself home alive, once again to face the kingdom of the mad.

CHAPTER 8

Distant Music

Distant Music he would call the picture if he were a painter.
James Joyce, "The Dead"

NINETEEN sixty-four was a crucial year in Joan Didion's literary career. Having just published *Run River*, she was afraid that she might never write another novel. "I sat in front of my typewriter," she tells us, "and believed that another subject would never present itself. I believed that I would be forever dry. I believed that I would 'forget how.' Accordingly, as a kind of desperate finger exercise, I tried writing stories."[1] She wrote three stories that year and—except for classroom exercises while at Berkeley—none in any other year. Indeed, she readily admits to having "no feel for the particular rhythms of short fiction, no ability to focus the world in the window" (*Stories*, p. 10), and tends—if anything—to be overly critical of her own work. Nevertheless, it seems to me that these three stories— "Coming Home" (*Saturday Evening Post*, July 11, 1964), "The Welfare Island Ferry," (*Harper's Bazaar*, June 1965), and "When Did Music Come This Way? Children Dear, Was It Yesterday?" (*Denver Quarterly*, Winter 1967)—merit our attention if only because of the insight they give us into their author's artistic development. For in Didion's stories we find some of the same themes which dominate her three novels.

Among the most nearly central of these themes is loss of home and of one's past. Just as the protagonists of her short stories are cut off from any sense of personal continuity, so too are the major characters in her novels victims of temporal provincialism[2] (the old-guard Californians in *Run River* experience the social convulsions which come with economic expansion; Maria Wyeth in *Play It as It Lays* suffers the trauma of seeing her childhood home become a guided-missile range; and Charlotte Douglas in *A Book of Common Prayer* abandons the familiar milieu of North America for the *terra incognita* of a banana republic near the Equator).

In addition, we see in Didion's fiction the continuation of a type of sexual conflict which pervades American literature. In *Love and Death in the American Novel* Leslie Fiedler speaks of this conflict in terms of the seeming schizophrenia which informs our perception of sexual identity.[3] Fiedler argues that just as women are frequently viewed as being either virgin or whore, earth mother or bitch goddess; so too are men often depicted in terms of two extremes—as being either gentleman or seducer, rational suitor or demon lover. (In pulp art these prototypes are crudely and obviously drawn, but in serious literature they achieve mythic proportions.) Accordingly, the protagonist in each of Didion's mature fictions is attracted to a male who is emotionally intemperate and—in some cases—even Dionysian in character. (Her novels, but not her stories, also feature a counter-balancing Apollonian figure.)[4] Yet the conflict which bedevils these protagonists is never satisfactorily resolved, for in Didion's fictional world no form of love can ultimately prevail. Indeed, if hell—as Dostoyevsky contends—is the inability to love, then Didion's women exist in an everlasting purgatory: capable of affection, they lack an external context within which that affection can be shown. To see that this is so, we need only turn to the individual works themselves.

The principal character in "Coming Home" is Mary Monroe Sweet, a free-lance writer possessed with "a gift for devising the kind of television drama known as 'controversial'" (p. 52). Mary is a young woman from Kentucky who lives in New York with her unemployed husband, Charlie Sloane. (Until recently, Charlie had worked as a story editor for a major television network.) Mary's writing occasionally takes her to California, and it is her return from one such trip which constitutes the dramatic situation of Didion's story.

This story opens with an acrimonious conversation between Mary and Charlie. (Didion's ear for the cadences of hostile dialogue and her feel for the dynamics of marital rancor is as unerring here as in her novels.) In the course of their quarrel we learn several things about these people. We learn that Mary has spent time in the hospital—probably because of a nervous breakdown—and that Charlie has had an affair during his wife's stay on the west coast. Finally, we learn that the Sloanes are to be parents, a prospect which Mary greets with equal measures of hope and apprehension and which Charlie fails even to acknowledge.

Like many of Didion's characters, Mary has lost touch with her past and has become an expatriate from her childhood home. She had been a scholarship student at Barnard when her father had died and she had returned home to see him laid to rest in that "Eastern

Kentucky town where he had for twenty years operated the Black Diamond Mine":

> "Teach us to number our days," the minister muttered in the Masonic Cemetery; touched, Mary Monroe's mother had numbered her days and found them unpromising, had deserted the grave that same afternoon and fled to kinder country, the Gulf Coast of Florida, where one month later she married a retired Air Force colonel and settled in a place named Sunshine Keys. . . . That spring it seemed to . . . [Mary] that there was no one left, since her mother's defection, to certify her childhood—no one who remembered the rabbit that froze to death or the night she woke screaming with an earache or the songs her father improvised about her on the Chickering in the dining room (*Pack up my sweet Mary Monroe, here we go, swingin' low, bye, bye, Mary*)—and therefore that in certain respects she had ceased to exist. (pp. 51–52)

Clearly, the title of this story is ironic in a number of ways. To begin with, Mary's childhood home in Kentucky is lost to her. She cannot go back there any more than Maria Wyeth in *Play It as It Lays* can return to her home in Nevada. Also, Mary's homecoming to New York—which is the literal reference of Didion's title—leads only to an exchange of recriminations with a callous and unfaithful husband. Indeed, she has lost even her sexual bond with that husband, for when Mary climbs into bed, exhausted from her trip, and asks Charlie to hold her for a while, he simply kisses her on the forehead and tells her that he has an early appointment downtown. Her anger and frustration are only partially mollified by a glass of Pernod and a couple of phenobarbitals.

Since her ties with both past and present are ephemeral at best, Mary's only solace lies in hope for the future. Like Maria Wyeth and like Charlotte Douglas, Mary defines that hope in terms of mother-hood. While still unmarried, "she pinned a baby-food advertisement beside her bed, and sometimes when she was tired and when Charlie Sloane had gone home she would lie in bed, staring into the baby's larger-than-life eyes and imagining that the baby was hers, forever to lie beside her. The baby never grew older, never had a father" (p. 55). For her this baby, forever secured in the fixity of art, represents a kind of emotional ballast in a world of otherwise mutable affections.

We last see Mary Monroe Sweet on the cold morning of her homecoming, lying numbly in bed—wrapped in a warm fog of pills and milky white liqueur. "When she was almost asleep she was able to conjure up the image of the baby, not her own unknown baby (she did not think about that) but the loved baby in the baby-food advertisement, and as she burrowed deeper under the blankets she imagined herself singing to that baby, day after shining day, singing until its larger-than-life eyes closed, just for her, *Pack up my sweet Mary Monroe, here we go, swingin' low, bye, bye, Mary*" (p. 55).

The themes of romantic discord and alienation from one's home recur in "The Welfare Island Ferry," the second of Joan Didion's stories from the 1960s and one of the works most representative of her fiction. We have here, as in so many of her other works, a bewildered and sensitive woman who has fallen under the spell of an alternately charming and malignant man. (We are told that whenever Miller Hardin entered a room "everyone seemed both delighted by his arrival and, because after a few drinks he would become abusive . . . , relieved by his departure" [p. 82].) The young woman in question—Miss Louisa Patterson Pool—is from Marin County, California; and her lover Miller Hardin, from Biloxi, Mississippi.[5]

Louisa and Miller meet at a Friday-night party early one spring.[6] She "had left that party with him for a larger party, and had woken through the weekend at various times of day and night in several apartments, in several states, on sofas and on beds and once on an old-fashioned porch glider that seemed to be, absurdly, on a terrace overlooking the East River" (p. 82). By Monday they arrive at an unspoken agreement to remain together and by June Louisa "was convinced that she, who had never before needed anyone, could not have slept without Miller Hardin" (p. 82).

On that first Monday Louisa and Miller end up in the West Village apartment of an absent woman. On the bathroom wall of that apartment Louisa sees a framed photograph of Miller, "an enlarged snapshot that showed him sitting in a lawn chair near a river" (p. 82). She imagines this picture to have been taken on the Eastern Shore of Maryland, because that region represents for her a kind of upper-class order and decorum. Like Mary Monroe Sweet, Louisa uses a photograph to connect herself imaginatively to a world which is both desired and pragmatically inaccessible.

As it turns out the apartment to which Miller has brought her belongs to his sister Barbara. He had found Barbara's unconscious body there on Friday morning and he had carried her to the hospital, where she had died before her stomach could be pumped. It is now Monday and a requiem Mass is to be said for Barbara at Saint Ignatius Loyola Church. (Because she was a suicide, Barbara could not be buried by the Church; but her "ex-husband had been able to arrange the mass" [p. 82].) As one might expect, Miller is out of place in church. He still remembers some surface amenities—he insists that Louisa find something with which to cover her head—but he slouches awkwardly in the pew, neither kneeling nor standing. And when the Mass is over, he says, "Have them do it again." "After he had repeated it twice and added 'Get me out of here, just get me the hell *out* of this,' Louisa led him stumbling, out of the church" (p. 82). As a southerner in New York and a nonpracticing Catholic, Miller Hardin is bereft of both a cultural and religious past.

The only past which Louisa has known consists of the lost world of her upper-middle-class Northern California childhood. She is able to get in touch with an east-coast equivalent of that lost world, however, when—at Miller's insistence—she spends a weekend on Long Island Sound with the family of "an old beau named Henry Taylor." Didion describes the Taylor home with a keen eye for detail:

There were moss roses in her bedroom and Porthault towels in the bathroom, and her hair curled from the damp in the air. Henry and Louisa and Henry's parents and thirteen-year-old twin sisters ate lobsters and long ears of corn at a trestle table in the garden where the moss roses grew, and no telephone rang. . . . The twins played the piano, "Blue Moon" and "Once in a While" and "Heart and Soul," demonstrating to Louisa how the chords coincided. . . . [This] was the world of her own adolescence, a world in which she could remember wanting nothing other than a peppermint-pink cashmere sweater and a collection of black bathing suits and a good baby-oil-and-iodine tan and enough privacy to neck on the chaise longue in the pool house. (p. 83)

By Sunday, however, the spell is broken. It is raining, a piano string has snapped, and the twins are arguing over a game of gin rummy. Louisa, knowing that it is time to leave, makes an excuse to return early to New York and to Miller.

When she gets back to her apartment the familiar, tired ritual of argument and complaint resumes. It seems that Miller and Louisa constantly talk about the value of making plans without ever really making any. To them the future appears strangely chimerical and problematic. Indeed, their final point of contention in the story involves Miller's spur-of-the-moment plan that they catch the last ferry to Welfare Island and back. Louisa reminds her lover that the Welfare Island Ferry has ceased to run. Had he not informed her of that fact himself a few days earlier? "All right," Miller replies. "All right. There never *was* a ferry to Welfare Island, I suppose. Have it your own way. And while you're at it *develop* some *character*, why don't you" (p. 107).

That night Louisa lies awake in Miller's arms thinking of all the places they will never go. She "thought about Washington and about Charlottesville, and about Chicago, where he had promised they might go when the heat broke. She even thought about her father and about California, where Miller had promised they might spend Christmas, and about Welfare Island, where she had not yet been. Miller had been there once, years ago; he had told her about it the week before." The story ends just before dawn when Miller whispers to Louisa, *"Hold onto me,"* and she does (p. 107).

As is the case with "Coming Home" and "The Welfare Island Ferry," "When Did Music Come This Way . . . ?" deals with a woman whose past and future seem distinctly unreal and who—in her own words—is trying desperately to "hold on" in the present. Didion's unnamed protagonist tells her story in the first person and addresses her reader directly. "I wish that memory made no connections," she says, "for I would like to tell you about it straight, would like you to see it as finished and self-contained as a painting on a gallery wall; would like you to interpret it to *me*" (p. 54). What she would like for the reader to interpret to her are the events of a Christmas evening during her childhood in Reno, 1945.

As a girl the narrator would celebrate Christmas with her family, a group which included her cousin Cary, her Aunt Inez, and whomever her Aunt Inez happened to be married to at the time. This particular Christmas Aunt Inez's husband is a flier named Ward. Ward is a heavy drinker who stays away for long periods of time and who does not arrive that Christmas until late on the night of the twenty-fifth. Earlier that evening the narrator and Cary had had an argument in the room which they were sharing. Cary is incensed by her stepfather's absence and maintains that she would never "marry someone like Ward" (p. 58). As the conversation progresses the narrator becomes increasingly peeved with her cousin. "I watched Cary pinning up the last strands of her hair, and wished again that I had hair like hers. 'Who you *plan*ning on marrying then?' I asked after a while. 'Frank Sinatra? Audie Murphy? Dr. Albert Schweitzer?'" And Cary replies: "'Never you mind. He won't stay away three days at a time on *Christ*mas, you can be sure. I guess I can call that tune'" (p. 59).

At this point the narrator lashes out at Cary with a gesture that is "stupid, blunted, vicious only in tone" (p. 59). "I cannot now tell you why I turned on Cary," she recalls, "for I loved her. Did we not share a grandmother, wear identical polo coats? Had we not spent Christmas together always? How could I have not loved her?" (p. 59). The narrator takes the music box which Cary had given her as a Christmas present and jams it against her cousin's ear. *"'You guess you can call that tune,'* I chanted, *'what tune is that, Cary, is this the tune?'"* (p. 59). Frightened, Cary wrenches the music box from her cousin and drops it. Neither of them moves as the box cracks and its works shatter and shoot across the floor, under the dressing table and the bed, and into the open closet. Cary is distraught at the fact that she has broken her cousin's music box, and even more distraught at the narrator's seeming indifference to the catastrophe. When her cousin's attempts to console her prove ineffectual, Cary locks herself in the bathroom and the narrator goes downstairs to sleep on the sofa behind the Christmas tree.

(The Christmas tree may be something of a symbol in this story. The large tree in the narrator's childhood home signified the solidarity of her family, precarious and seasonal though that solidarity may have been. However, the tree in her present apartment has lost almost all its needles and is adorned with strings of broken ornaments. Moreover, it is a fire hazard and her husband has threatened to call the fire department if the narrator does not have it removed.)

After she has been on the sofa for a while the narrator notices Ward and Aunt Inez sitting across the room, visible through the branches of the tree. "I do not remember all they said," she tells us, "not only because I was half asleep but because they repeated the same things over and over, words that meant nothing to me,[7] fragments of sentences they seemed to have begun so many times before that there was no need to finish them" (p. 60). Ward leans close to his wife and says, "'Tell me, Inez. Tell me how much. Tell me what you'd do.' 'Anything,' Aunt Inez said again and again. 'You know what I'd do. Anything'" (p. 61). The interrogation proceeds despite Inez's pleas that Ward stop:

"Tell me what you'd do for it."
. . . .

"I'd do anything," she repeated.
"Say it out loud. Who would you betray."
"I can't tonight."
"Say it."
There was a silence, and then Aunt Inez said, as if by rote, "I would betray my mother. I would betray my sister. I would betray Cary."
"OK," Ward said softly then, and sat back. "OK." (p. 61)

Throughout the remainder of the story we get periodic glimpses of the narrator's present life. We learn, for example, that she is estranged from her philandering husband, Charlie. Possessing the same first name and the same personality as Mary Monroe Sweet's husband, Charlie is the sort of individual who awakens his wife at four in the morning by throwing snow on her bed. (The fit of pique with which she responds to this childish prank reminds the narrator of her attack on Cary: as Charlie "pointed out before he left, I didn't even get the name right. I said everything that was ugly and nothing that hit the mark" [p. 59].) In the intervening years Ward has died— killed in a South Dakota aerial show in 1949—and Aunt Inez has never remarried. The narrator tells us at the outset of the story that— at thirty-three—she has reached the age, "as has Cary," where two drinks before lunch can blur her looks (p. 54). And at the end of the story we learn that she recently has had lunch with her cousin. Cary, who has married twice, "had five vodka martinis, one in lieu of dessert" (p. 61).

Probably the most puzzling question that arises concerning this story involves the meaning of its title. "When did music come this way?/Children dear, was it yesterday?" is a line from Matthew Arnold's poem "The Forsaken Merman." This poem is a monologue in which the speaker—a mythic creature from the sea—laments the fact that his human wife, Margaret, has deserted him and their children to return to her former home on land. Certain rough parallels with Didion's story immediately suggest themselves. To begin with Inez, though she may never actually desert her family, does concede to Ward her willingness to do so. (However—unlike the merman's wife—who is lured away from her maternal loyalty by church bells, Inez is prey to a more elemental temptation.) Also, one of the most memorable scenes in Arnold's poem follows the merman and his children from the sea to the village church where they find the praying Margaret, her eyes fixed not on them but "seal'd to the holy book." Similarly, the denouement of Didion's story occurs when the narrator gazes undetected at Aunt Inez paying obeisance to Ward. Indeed, the repetitive, ritualistic quality of their conversation is not unlike that of a private liturgy.

Another line of speculation might identify Ward with the merman, himself. There is a kind of mythic aloofness about Ward. He is removed from the rest of the family, the narrator tells us. "I do not mean that he disliked us; we simply failed to touch him" (pp. 56–57). And when she tries to think of Ward she "can call up only cartoon characters: Smilin' Jack, Steve Canyon, the nameless flier in love with Lace" (p. 56). (Finally, Ward is like Arnold's merman in that neither is at home on earth: one swims in the sea, the other soars on the air.) We ought not to push this comparison too far, however. Margaret forsakes the merman as well as her children, whereas Ward is Inez's sole focus of fidelity, the person for whom she would betray all others.

Perhaps the safest assertion we can make here is that the sense of nostalgia, loss, and pathos which characterizes Arnold's poem conveys precisely the tone which Didion seeks in her story. By alluding to "The Forsaken Merman" in her title she may be attempting to deepen the resonance of that tone. And more concretely, we can see the breaking of the music box as a symbolic sundering of the harmonies of childhood and of home.[8] When did music come this way? Perhaps it was yesterday, surely not today, probably not tomorrow.

CHAPTER 9

What "Nothing" Means

INCREASING attention has been paid in recent years to the element of regionalism in Hollywood literature. Among those studies which immediately come to mind are Jonas Spatz's *Hollywood in Fiction: Some Versions of the American Myth* (1969), Walter Wells's *Tycoons and Locusts* (1973), Tom Dardis's *Some Time in the Sun* (1976), and individual biographies of Nathanael West (by Jay Martin, 1970), John O'Hara (by Matthew J. Bruccoli, 1975), and Raymond Chandler (by Frank MacShane, 1976). In a sense Joan Didion is also part of the Hollywood literary tradition: she has spent most of her career in the Southern California that Walter Wells calls Southland; she has worked in and written about the motion picture industry; and—in *Play It as It Lays*—she has given us a strangely ironic perspective on classic Southland nihilism. In order to understand the thematic importance of Hollywood to her writing, however, we need first to understand the archetypal significance of Hollywood to the American experience in general.

In his book Spatz sees Hollywood as both the geographic and mythic culmination of America's movement westward. He writes: "Hollywood, as the western boundary of the frontier movement, is the land of abundance and growth, of sunshine and eternal spring. Its motion pictures recapture the optimism and moral certainty of a vanished age, and its movie stars symbolize a vanished innocence. . . . The vision of Hollywood is born of expectation and disappointment, external success and inner failure. The tone of the Hollywood novel, as a result, is frequently ironic and angry, and its ambivalent imagery reflects all the contradictions of the American myth" (p. 116). The dominant irony in Hollywood fiction, then, does not derive from the collapse of an existing social order—as is the case with southern literature and with *Run River*—but from the dissolution of an old myth, of what used to be called "the American dream." Indeed, Walter Wells contends that at the very center of Hollywood fiction there is "a theme of *dissolution*, a generalized breaking down of the old, the traditional, the real and the substantive" (p. 12). And the Hollywood novel, it seems to me, treats this theme of dissolution in a number of specific ways.

To begin with, we find in Southland fiction a persistent inversion of reality. The dominant symbol of pretense here is, of course, the motion picture industry. Throughout the Hollywood novel movies function in much the same way as did the theater trope in earlier dramatic literature; and even in those novels which are only marginally concerned with film-making, a meretricious ambience nevertheless pervades. In Nathanael West's *The Day of the Locust*, for example, we read of a fat lady in a yachting cap who is "going shopping, not boating"; of a man in a Norfolk jacket and Tyrolean hat who is "returning, not from a mountain, but an insurance office"; and of a girl wearing slacks and sneakers and a bandanna, who has "just left a switchboard, not a tennis court" (*Works*, p. 261). Such figures, however, are not mere metaphorical constructs, but individuals whom one might have encountered in the Hollywood of West's time, or, as Allan Seager puts it, "not fantasy imagined but fantasy seen."[1]

What we have here is a sort of reverse mimesis in which life imitates art. A particularly grotesque example of this phenomenon can be found in another scene from West's novel. Here Tod, Faye, and Homer listen to a female impersonator—in evening gown—sing a lullaby. "He had a soft, throbbing voice," West writes, "and his gestures were matronly, tender and aborted, a series of unconscious caresses. What he was doing was in no sense parody. . . . This dark young man with his thin hairless arms and soft, rounded shoulders, who rocked an imaginary cradle as he crooned, was really a woman." Upon finishing, "the young man . . . became an actor again. He tripped on his train, as though he weren't used to it, lifted his skirts to show he was wearing Paris garters, then strode off swinging his shoulders. His imitation of a man was awkward and obscene" (p. 370).

As one might infer from the foregoing, Southland fiction not only inverts reality but it jettisons conventional norms of sexuality as well. Surely it is no accident that Norman Mailer entitled his Hollywood novel *The Deer Park*. Named after the erotic playground of Louis XV, this novel depicts meaningless promiscuity and the perversion of normal physical lust. (Indeed, one of Mailer's major characters— Marion Faye—is a homosexual, a pimp, and a sadist.) If the modern world is one in which traditional notions of romance have been replaced by a freer sensuality, then the world of Hollywood-Southland has taken us one step further—from sophistication to decadence.

Also, we encounter in the Hollywood novel the utter failure of subjective rituals to fill the vacuum created by the loss of objective structures of meaning. This failure is singularly evident in the tawdry Southland milieu of Evelyn Waugh's *The Loved One*. Waugh's brutal satire is not directed merely at the excesses of the funeral industry, but also at the spiritually eviscerating effects of secular materialism. (He seems to be saying that our hysteria to camouflage the reality of death stems from the anxiety that life itself is less than real; for if we acknowledge death as the end of life, we must assess the significance of that which is ended.) It may well be that the spiritual under-pinnings of our age have given way less from cataclysmic assault than from gradual attenuation. Indeed, when Waugh's Dennis Barlow decides to become a nonsectarian clergyman, he asks—apparently with a straight face, "Is there a non-sectarian bishop who ordains you?"[2]

Ideally, rituals and the values which they embody provide a context for our present existence. Spiritual dissolution, however, results in the erosion of that context. Cut off from both past and future, one is cruelly isolated and effectively dehumanized. Allen Tate refers to such a condition as the "new provincialism." "The provincial attitude," he writes, "is limited in time but not in space." The new provincial "cuts himself off from the past, and without benefit of the fund of traditional wisdom approaches the simplest problems of life as if nobody had ever heard of them before" (*Essays*, p. 593). In the solipsistic milieu of Hollywood-Southland this new provincialism is the temporal norm. And it is perhaps fitting that one of the purest examples of the conflict between this norm and that of the old traditionalism is depicted in a story called "Golden Land," by an obscure Hollywood fictionist named William Faulkner.

The protagonist of Faulkner's story—Ira Ewing—leaves Nebraska for Los Angeles at age fourteen. In the ensuing thirty-four years he becomes a successful real-estate agent and an alcoholic; he fathers a son and a daughter—a homosexual and a prostitute, respectively; and he moves his aging mother west to die. Mrs. Ewing, however, is not content to remain in California and throughout the story she tries to save enough money to return to Nebraska. Since Ira will not allow her to handle large sums of money and since the train fare is always a bit more than the amounts she can furtively scrape together, her plans are consistently thwarted. Still, Mrs. Ewing has one advantage over her son—she is trapped only by space, not by time. (Indeed, when Ira reminds her that *his* children were born in California, she replies, "Just one generation. The generation before that they were born in a sodroofed dugout on the Nebraska wheat frontier. And the one before that in a log house in Missouri. And the one before that in a Kentucky blockhouse with Indians around it."[3]) It may be that in the contrast between Mrs. Ewing's firm sense of her own heritage and her son's utter rootlessness Faulkner is doing what Didion would do a few decades later—he is constructing a paradigm for life in the golden land.

True to the new provincialism, Ira is cut off from the future as well as from the past. In one of the most vivid scenes in the story he sits with his middle-aged mistress, watching young people on the beach: "young men in trunks, and young girls in little more, with bronzed, unselfconscious bodies. . . . They seemed to him to walk along the rim of the world as though they and their kind alone inhabited it, and he with his forty-eight years were the forgotten lost survivor of another race and kind, and they in turn precursors of a new race not yet seen on the earth: of men and women without age, beautiful as gods and goddesses, and with the minds of infants" (p. 721).

I   *Not Exactly Locusts*

Joan Didion might well be described as an antielitist film critic. Although she is hardly an unblinking apologist for Hollywood, she has little regard for the rarefied tastes of such fashionable critics as Stanley Kauffmann, John Simon, and Pauline Kael.[4] In reading through her movie reviews, particularly her regular column for *Vogue* (January 1, 1964—February 15, 1966), one is struck by their author's willingness to defend the popular and to attack the chic: she praises *Dr. Zhivago* and *The Unsinkable Molly Brown*, while finding serious fault with Carl Foreman's *The Victors* and Sidney Lumet's *The Pawnbroker*. (And more recently in "Letter from 'Manhattan'" she is severely critical of a heralded director of much later vintage—Woody Allen.[5]) In the first of her *Vogue* columns Didion is abundantly clear as to the sorts of films she admires. "I make excuses to be at home," she writes, "whenever Wendell Corey is slithering in and out of *The Big Knife* on the Late Show; I pull up the covers and settle in with mindless delight when Katherine Hepburn sweeps into *The Philadelphia Story.* I weep when James Stewart brings *The Spirit of St. Louis* in over the coast of Ireland, weep when Joel McCrea tells America how The Lights Are Going Out All Over Europe Tonight in *Foreign Correspondent;* weep even when James Mason flounders into the surf at Malibu in the Judy Garland *A Star Is Born*" (p. 24).

Eclipsing all other affections, however, is the author's love for John

Wayne. Her review of Wayne's *The Alamo* (*National Review*, December 31, 1960) may dutifully note that movie's shortcomings, but it also acknowledges the Duke's proprietary claim on Miss Didion's tear ducts. She tells us that she "wept as Wayne told his Mexican inamorata How A Man's Gotta Live . . . , wept as he explained why Republic Is A Beautiful Word." "So conspicuous was my sniffling," she continues, "that you could scarcely hear the snickers from my neighbors, a couple of young men from *Esquire*, both of whom resembled Arthur M. Schlesinger Jr." And she ruefully maintains, "They don't make 'em like Duke on the New Frontiers" (p. 415).

Although we can infer much about Didion's attitude toward Hollywood from her reaction to specific films, we do not need to rely on such indirect methods of analysis. Her essays "In Hollywood" (*Album*, pp. 153–67) and "I Can't Get That Monster Out of My Mind" (*Slouching*, pp. 149–56)[6] focus directly on the motion picture industry. And the view of that industry which she presents is so balanced and so judicious as to constitute revisionist history.

In the first of the essays mentioned above she advances the unconventional notion that Hollywood is "the last extant stable society." "This is a community," she writes, "whose notable excesses include virtually none of the flesh or the spirit: heterosexual adultery is less easily tolerated than respectably settled homosexual marriages or well-managed liaisons between middle-aged women. . . . Flirtations between men and women, like drinks after dinner, remain largely the luxury of character actors out from New York, one-shot writers, reviewers being courted by Industry people, and others who do not understand the *mise* of the local *scene*" (pp. 154–55). The source of stability—the very raison d'etre—of this society is not sex, or money, or even fame, but rather the architectonics of the deal itself. Didion observes:

The place makes everyone a gambler. Its spirit is speedy, obsessive, immaterial. The action itself is the art form, and is described in aesthetic terms: "A very imaginative deal," they say, or "He writes the most creative deals in the business." There is in Hollywood, as in all cultures in which gambling is the central activity, a lowered sexual energy, an inability to devote more than token attention to the preoccupations of the society outside. The action is everything, more consuming than sex, more immediate than politics; more important always than the acquisition of money, which is never, for the gambler, the true point of the exercise. (*Album*, pp. 159–60)

The author goes on to speak of legendary checks which float around the Industry like Monopoly money. An agent tells her that he has on his desk a check made out for $1,275,000, "the client's share of first profits on a picture now in release." The previous week she had seen "another such check, this one made out for $4,850,000." "In a curious way," she writes, "these checks are not 'real,' not real money in the sense that a check for a thousand dollars can be real money; no one 'needs' $4,850,000, nor is it really disposable income. . . . But the actual pieces of paper which bear such figures have, in the community, a totemic significance" (p. 160).

Finally, the aesthetics of the deal makes film criticism a chancy and ephemeral undertaking. "A finished picture defies all attempts to analyze what makes it work or not work: the responsibility for its every frame is clouded not only in the accidents and compromises of production but in the clauses of its financing. . . . Some reviewers make a point of trying to understand whose picture it is by 'looking at the script': to understand whose picture it is one needs to look not particularly at the script but at the deal memo" (p. 165). The reason for this confusion is that frequently motion picture production is less the result of collaboration than of protracted conflict. It is often as important to know who has the final cut on a film as it is to know who conceived the original story.

"I Can't Get That Monster Out of My Mind" (1964) predates "In Hollywood" by nine years; however, the sentiments expressed in the former essay are similar to those found in the latter one.[7] In much the same way as Tom Dardis would do several years later in *Some Time in the Sun*, Didion begins her discussion in "Monster" by challenging certain derogatory myths about Hollywood. One such myth is that of "Hollywood the Destroyer." "In the popular imagination," she writes,

the American motion picture industry still represents a kind of mechanical monster, programmed to stifle and destroy all that is interesting and worthwhile and "creative" in the human spirit. . . . Mention Hollywood, and we are keyed to remember Scott Fitzgerald, dying at Malibu, attended only by Sheilah Graham while he ground out college-weekend movies (he was also writing *The Last Tycoon*, but that is not part of the story); we are conditioned to recall the brightest minds of a generation, deteriorating around the swimming pool at the Garden of Allah while they waited for calls from the Thalberg Building. (p. 150)[8]

Surprisingly, it is not just exquisitely sensitive poseurs, but also the Industry itself, which has helped to foster the anti-Hollywood myth. Didion speaks of Industry people who complain about the long-term dominance of the major studios and about the relative difficulty of articulating an "individual voice" in American motion pictures. She contends that "these protests have about them an engaging period optimism, depending as they do upon the Rousseauean premise that most people, left to their own devices, think not in clichés but with originality and brilliance; that most individual voices, once heard, turn out to be voices of beauty and wisdom" (p. 152). Unfortunately, the truth is often otherwise.

One reason why this is so is that "American directors, with a handful of exceptions, are not much interested in style . . . , [but] are at heart didactic" (p. 153). Thus, when they *are* given a chance to make a personal statement the result is all too often an exercise in moral pomposity. As an example Didion cites Stanley Kramer's *Judgment at Nuremberg*. This film, made in 1961, "was an intrepid indictment not of authoritarianism in the abstract, not of the trials themselves, not of the various moral and legal issues involved, but of Nazi war atrocities, about which there would have seemed already to be some consensus." "(You may remember" [Didion notes parenthetically] "that *Judgment at Nuremberg* received an Academy Award, which the screenwriter Abby Mann accepted on the behalf of 'all intellectuals')" (p. 154).

For years critics of the Hollywood "monster" have yearned for the time when we would have fewer and better films. Didion concludes that we now have fewer films but not necessarily better ones. However, the fault may not lie with the "monster" itself, so much as with the creative banality of many who seek to realize their private fantasies on the motion picture screen. "Not long ago I met a producer," she tells us, "who complained to me of the difficulties he had working within what I recognized as the System, although he did not call it that. He longed, he said, to do an adaptation of a certain Charles Jackson short story. 'Some really terrific stuff,' he said. 'Can't touch it, I'm afraid. About masturbation'" (p. 156).

II *The Still Center of Day*

Despite the image of the movie capital which we find in Didion's Hollywood essays, the ambience of *Play It as It Lays* is anything but that of the "last extant stable society." Instead, we have in this novel the tawdry and nihilistic setting of traditional Southland fiction, a setting where the cultural disintegration which began to occur in *Run River* is already an accomplished fact. Here a young, marginal actress named Maria Wyeth drives the Los Angeles freeways in a Corvette.

Here, only the ritual of making complicated lane changes can bring order to an otherwise chaotic life.

Maria is originally from Silver Wells, Nevada, a former mining community that is now the site of a nuclear test range. She is separated from her obnoxiously cruel husband—Carter Lang—and from her institutionalized, retarded daughter, Kate. (Indeed, the only thing that holds any meaning for Maria is her maternal love for Kate; and given Kate's condition and circumstances, there is little chance that that love can either be demonstrated or returned.) When Maria once again becomes pregnant (probably not by her husband), Carter pressures her into having an abortion by threatening that he will otherwise prevent her from seeing Kate. Following her abortion, and other lesser traumas, Maria finds herself—at the end of the novel— assisting a suicide. Her friend—Carter's producer BZ—climbs into bed with her, swallows a handful of Seconal, and dies in Maria's comforting arms. But unlike BZ, Maria keeps on living.

Told in eighty-seven chapters, covering 214 pages, Maria's story is one of psychic collapse. Along with the image of void suggested by the abundance of white space on many of the novel's pages,[9] the sense of fragmentation conveyed by the short, staccato chapters (some as short as a single paragraph) reminds us of the spiritual chaos foretold in the Yeats poem from which Didion derived the title of *Slouching Towards Bethlehem*. As Guy Davenport points out, "she has given the novel a pace so violent and so powerful that its speed becomes the dominant symbol of her story."[10]

The narrative focus of Didion's second novel is more limited, and hence more controlled, than that of *Run River*. (Indeed, Alfred Kazin argues that in *Play It as It Lays* "Joan Didion is too much in control . . . , literally the director-*auteur*, as they now say in cinema circles.") The novel begins with respective first-person accounts by Maria, by BZ's wife, Helene, and by Carter and ends with a final word from Maria; however, the bulk of the story is told from a third-person limited perspective. Formalistically, the first-person narrations are surely the weakest part of this novel. Kazin is right to point out that "Maria would hardly ask . . . 'Why should a coral snake need two glands of neurotoxic poison to survive while a king snake, *so similarly marked*, needs none. Where is the Darwinian logic there?'"[11] Still, these first-person monologues constitute a relatively small proportion of the entire novel. The third-person point of view, which is much more effective, is also far more dominant. Through it Didion is able to move quite easily from a close identification with Maria to an ironic distance from her. At times we are painfully close to Maria's troubled psyche and at other times the cool, objective voice of Didion's narrator can be heard, moderating the confusion and panic of Maria's story with an icily mordant wit.

On occasion, however, the process works the other way around. Consider, for example, Chapter 48. Here the narration begins rather cattily: "There was at first that spring an occasional faggot who would take her to parties. Never a famous faggot, never one of those committed months in advance to escorting the estranged wives of important directors, but a third-string faggot. At first she was even considered a modest asset by several of them. . . . She understood, for example, about shoes, and could always distinguish from among the right bracelet and the amusing impersonation of the right bracelet and the bracelet that was merely a witless copy" (p. 125).[12] But by the end of the chapter Maria's grief for her aborted child brings on a subliminal sense of dread: "She was drinking a good deal in the evenings now because when she drank she did not dream. 'This way to the gas, ladies and gentlemen,' a loudspeaker kept repeating in her dreams now, and she wold be checking off names as the children filed past her, the little children in the green antechamber, she would be collecting their lockets and baby rings in a fine mesh basket. Her instructions were to whisper a few comforting words to those children who cried or held back, because this was a humane operation" (p. 126).

Although the motion picture industry plays only a marginal role in this novel, Didion does employ the cinema trope for specific thematic purposes.[13] The two movies which Maria makes constitute a definite case in point. The first of these—a *cinéma vérité* picture called *Maria*—follows its subject around New York, showing her "asleep on a couch at a party . . . , on the telephone arguing with the billing department at Bloomingdale's . . . , cleaning some marijuana with a kitchen strainer . . . , crying on the IRT. At the end she was thrown into negative and looked dead" (p. 20). This film runs for seventy-four minutes, has won a prize at a festival in Eastern Europe, and has never been released. Her second picture—*Angel Beach*—is a bike movie in which she is raped by the members of a motorcycle gang. Maria enjoys watching this second film because "the girl on the screen seemed to have a definite knack for controlling her own destiny" (p. 20); whereas she feels that the girl in the first picture "had no knack for anything" (p. 21).

Like so many within the moral environment of Hollywood, Maria comes to define herself in terms of artifice. Just as the protagonist of Walker Percy's *The Moviegoer* uses motion pictures to "certify" his own mundane reality,[14] so too does Maria derive a certain fleeting comfort from seeing images of herself on the screen. (When she is staying in a furnished apartment after her abortion, she is able to sleep only after seeing herself in a television drama.) And when she thinks of the happy family that she and Carter and Kate will never be, she thinks in cinematic terms: "Carter throwing a clear plastic ball filled with confetti, Kate missing the ball. Kate crying. Carter swinging Kate by her wrists. The spray from the sprinklers and the clear plastic ball with the confetti falling inside and Kate's fat arms stretched up again for the catch she would always miss. Freeze frame. . . . On film they might have seemed a family" (pp. 137–38).

Maria faces a forbidding future unsustained by any vital connection with her past. When she is nine her father loses his house in a card game and the family moves from Reno to the smaller Nevada town of Silver Wells ("pop. then 28, now 0," p. 5). A prospective boom town that never materialized, Silver Wells is now a barren desert, a test range for doomsday weapons. Indeed, Maria's ties with her past have been so irrevocably severed that she is unable to "go back" even under hypnosis.

Maria's only link with her childhood comes through intermittent encounters with her late father's business partner, Benny Austin. At one point in the novel she runs into Benny in Las Vegas; however, this brush with her past is too much for Maria to cope with. As Benny orders them both Cuba Libres—a drink which she cannot remember anyone but her parents and Benny ever ordering—he proceeds to talk about *"as it was."* And she quietly slips out on him. She can even imagine him waiting there all night. "Benny would lay anybody in the Flamingo five-to-one that Harry and Francine Wyeth's daughter would not run out on him, and five-to-one were the best odds Benny would lay on the sun rising" (p. 148).

Later in the novel Maria tries vainly to get in touch with this surrogate-father. When she finds that his phone is no longer in service, she sends a letter to his post office box and sits next to the box for three days, waiting for someone to come. Finally a woman arrives, disclaims knowledge of "any Benny person," and accuses Maria of tampering with the U.S. Mail. Then the woman's face turns white and her voice rises: "You're Luanne's foster mother, is exactly who you are, and you're nosing around Vegas because you heard about the injury settlement, well just you *forget* it. I said *forget it*" (pp. 167–68). Maria's search for a father runs into a dead-end as she encounters a virtual parody of maternal suspicion and recrimination.

Just as elusive as her quest for familial affection is Maria's desire for sexual fulfillment. One of the more harrowing scenes in the novel occurs when she attends a typically decadent Hollywood party and goes to bed with an egocentric young actor named Johnny Waters. Didion describes the scene:

When they finally did it they were on the bed and at the moment before he came he reached under the pillow and pulled out an amyl nitrite popper and broke it under his nose, breathed in rapidly, and closed his eyes.
"Don't move," he said. *"I said don't move."*
Maria did not move.
"Terrific," he said then. His eyes were still closed.
Maria said nothing.
"Wake me up in three hours," he said. "With your tongue." (p. 153)

The copulation of Maria Wyeth and Johnny Waters hardly exemplifies the sort of redemptive sexual love envisioned by a D. H. Lawrence. (According to Norman Mailer, Lawrence believed "after every bitterness and frustration . . . that the physical love of men and women, insofar as it was untainted by civilization, was the salvation of us all."[15]) Instead, it reminds one of the bored assignation between Eliot's clerk-typist and the "young man carbuncular." We have gone beyond sexual iconoclasm here, to a sort of obsessive and joyless onanism.[16]

Like Lily McClellan, Maria is tormented by the uncertainties of love. Just as Lily is torn between the essentially benign and rational Everett and the destructive, charismatic Ryder Channing, so too is Maria bedeviled by different types of sexual attachment. Although she consciously eschews sadomasochism, her continuing dependence on Carter seems more than a little perverse. Also, her relationship with the obscurely demonic Ivan Costello suggests that Maria is used to being degraded and may secretly enjoy it.[17] And yet, from time to time, she entertains the hope of finding a more serene love with the basically kind-natured Les Goodwin.

After her abortion she fantasizes an idyllic life in which she and Kate and Les live in a house by the sea: "The house was like none she had ever seen but she thought of it so often that she knew even where the linens were kept, the plates, knew how the wild grass ran down to the beach and where the rocks made tidal pools" (p. 114). She and Kate would gather mussels on the beach and then later the three of them would sit at a big pine table "and Maria would light a kerosene lamp and they would eat the mussels and drink a bottle of cold white wine and after a while it would be time to lie down again, on the clean white sheets" (p. 114). "But by dawn she was always back in the house in Beverly Hills, uneasy in the queer early light . . . , [where she understood] that the still center of the daylight world was never a house by the sea but the corner of Sunset and La Brea. In that empty sunlight Kate could do no lessons, and the mussels on any shore that Maria knew were toxic" (p. 115).

When Maria and Les finally do spend a weekend together, the experience proves empty. They drive up the coast one night until they are exhausted. Then they sleep "wrapped together like children in a room by the sea in Morro Bay" (p. 133). Later they discuss various ways of spending their remaining time together. They could go up the coast to Big Sur, have a picnic, stay in the lodge; they could buy a sleeping bag and sleep on the beach. But they conclude that there is no point in doing any of these things. Didion sets the scene for this conclusion with a narrative paragraph whose force and concision are reminiscent of the style of her early model Hemingway: "*She dressed with her back to him,* then left the motel room and walked down to the water. A culvert had washed out and the equipment brought in to lift it was mired in the sandy mud. Bare-legged and bare-armed, shivering in her cotton jersey dress, she stood for a while watching them try to free the equipment. When she got back to the motel he was dressed, sitting on the unmade bed" [italics added] (p. 134).

Afterwards, Maria and Les make up any number of reasons for the failure of their tryst: "it had been the wrong time, the wrong place . . . [but] it would be all right another time, idyllic later. . . . They mentioned Kate, Carter, [Les's wife] Felicia, the weather, Oxnard, his dislike of motel rooms, her fear of subterfuge. They mentioned everything but one thing: that she had left the point in a bedroom in Encino" (pp. 134, 135). Of course, what Maria had left in the bedroom in Encino were the remains of her unborn child.

The significance not only of love, but also of death—and, hence, of life itself—is devalued in the spiritual wasteland which Didion's characters inhabit. This devaluation is brought into sharp focus in those chapters dealing with Maria's abortion. Here the elements of sexual perversion and of temporal provincialism come together. Such a nexus, however, is not unusual in the Hollywood novel. Although procreation traditionally has been seen as a means of improving as well as of perpetuating the species, the world of Southland fiction is such as to render both objectives nugatory. (In a nihilistic world the hope for human improvement is clearly ludicrous, while the perpetuation of a doomed species would be unthinkably cruel.) Accordingly, Maria cuts herself off from the future by aborting the new life within her.[18]

Maria's contact with the man who is to take her to the abortionist is made at a Thriftimart—under the big red T. (This ironically debased religious emblem pervades the landscape of Southern California in much the same way as the face of Dr. T. J. Eckleburg dominates that of Fitzgerald's Long Island.) When Maria meets her contact—a moral zombie in white duck pants—he begins to make inane smalltalk. Speaking of the neighborhood through which they are driving, he says: "Nice homes here. Nice for kids" (p. 78). He then asks Maria whether she gets good mileage on her car and proceeds to compare the merits of his Cadillac with those of a Camaro he is contemplating buying: "Maybe that sounds like a step down, a Cad to a Camaro, but I've got my eye on this *par*ticular Camaro, exact model of the pace car in the Indianapolis 500" (p. 79). The "conversation" continues in this vein until they pull into the abortionist's driveway. Then "Maria turned off the ignition and looked at the man in the white duck pants with an intense and grateful interest. In the past few minutes he had significantly altered her perception of reality: she saw now that she was not a woman on her way to have an abortion. She was a woman parking a Corvette outside a tract house while a man in white pants talked about buying a Camaro. There was no more to it than that" (p. 79).

Maria carries the spiritual wound of her experience with her long after the physical operation is over. (This point is emphasized in the film version of *Play It as It Lays* by the fact that Maria's purpose in going to a hypnotist is to find out whether foetuses think.) She is haunted by visions of the destroyed placenta coming back to her through the plumbing in her house, and eventually she moves into a furnished apartment. "But the next morning when the shower seemed slow to drain she threw up in the toilet, and after she had stopped trembling packed the few things she had brought to Fountain Avenue and, in the driving rain, drove back to the house in Beverly Hills. There would be plumbing anywhere she went" (p. 104). And one day, months later, she impulsively breaks into tears "because this was the day, the day the baby would have been born" (p. 141).

The attenuation of religious faith is hardly a dominant motif in Didion's novel. (Perhaps God has receded so far from the modern consciousness that it is pointless either to praise or curse His name.) However, a few religious implications do suggest themselves. Consider, for example, the pronunciation of Maria's name. "My name is Maria Wyeth," she says. "That is pronounced Mar-eye-ah, to get it straight at the outset" (p. 4). (The Blessed Virgin, however, is addressed: "Ave Ma-ree-ah.") Also, as David J. Geherin points out, when Maria wants to hear a human voice she calls dial-a-prayer.[19]

And finally, toward the end of the novel, she encounters a true believer—a woman sweeping sand outside a desert coffee shop. As the woman sweeps her sand into little piles, new sand blows in to take its place. The woman pauses from what Geherin notes are Sisyphean labors to ask Maria if she has made a decision: "I made my decision in '61 at a meeting in Barstow," the woman says, "and I never shed a tear since." "'No,' Maria said, 'I never did that'" (p. 199).

Living in a world of spiritual and cultural anomie, Maria does her best to cope with life on its own terms. In a way she is like Hemingway's Brett Ashley. Just as Brett tells Jake Barnes that deciding not to be a bitch is "sort of what we have instead of God," so too does Maria replace an absent deity[20] with certain quasi-ethical precepts: "She would never: *walk through the Sands or Caesar's alone after midnight.* She would never: *ball at a party, do S-M unless she wanted to, borrow furs from Abe Lipsey, deal.* She would never: *carry a Yorkshire in Beverly Hills*" (p. 136).

If there is one general principle which informs Maria's approach to the world, it is suggested by the title of Didion's novel. *"Always when I play back my father's voice,"* Maria tells us, *"it is with a professional rasp, it goes as it lays, don't do it the hard way. My father advised me that life itself was a crap game: it was one of the two lessons I learned as a child. The other was that overturning a rock was apt to reveal a rattlesnake. As lessons go those two seem to hold up, but not to apply"* (p. 200).

In expecting to find a snake under every rock, Maria is symbolically acknowledging the pervasiveness of evil in an essentially hostile universe. (She has suggested earlier that it is a universe in which one cannot even count on Darwinian logic to prevail.) So how does one live in such an environment? By playing it as it lays, by never taking the hard way in anything. Although Maria has learned this lesson in childhood and continues to live by it, she concedes that such stoic acceptance (if that is what it is) doesn't really work. It is simply one arbitrary method among many for dealing with the void in which we are doomed to live. (It is a lesson which seems to hold up *"but not to apply."*)

The action of *Play It as It Lays* concludes with BZ's suicide. If, as Albert Camus argues, the only serious philosophical problem is "judging whether life is or is not worth living,"[21] BZ, in doing away with himself, resolves this problem in the negative. He tells Maria, "You're still playing. . . . Some day you'll wake up and you just won't feel like playing any more" (p. 212). BZ sees suicide as a last significant act of defiance, a ritual of self-annihilation.[22] If life cannot be improved, he seems to say, then at least it can be ended. But for Maria such an attitude amounts to a pathetic kind of pose; or, as she says to BZ, "a queen's way of doing it" (p. 212).

Unlike BZ Maria is averse to examining life, philosophically or otherwise. (At the outset of the novel she says, "What makes Iago evil? some people ask. I never ask" [p. 3].) She tells us that she keeps on living only because she hopes some day to get Kate back and to go someplace where they can live simply. Maria will do some canning and be a mother to her child. (Significantly, her pastoral dream no longer includes Les Goodwin.) This hope is encouraging, however, only if there is a chance that it might be realized. Yet, by the end of the novel, we understand that Maria's dream is—in fact—hopeless. Viewed in this light, the closing lines of *Play It as It Lays* seem ironic indeed. Maria tells us,

> *I know something Carter never knew, or Helene, or maybe you. I know what "nothing" means, and keep on playing.*
> *Why, BZ would say.*
> *Why not, I say.* (p. 214)

Maria may actually believe that she is living for Kate; however, the truth—as Didion's narrative perspective forces us to see it—is that Maria continues to live because she does not even share BZ's faith in the meaningfulness of death.

(John Barth's Todd Andrews comes to much the same conclusion at the end of *The Floating Opera*. Todd writes in his journal: *"There's no final reason for living [or for suicide]."* And a bit later he says: "To realize that nothing makes any final difference is overwhelming; but if one goes no farther and becomes a saint, a cynic, or a suicide on principle, one hasn't reasoned completely. The truth is that nothing makes any difference, including that truth. Hamlet's question is, absolutely, meaningless."[23])

If we look closely at the final exchange which Maria imagines between herself and BZ, some interesting implications suggest themselves. In George Bernard Shaw's *Back to Methuselah* the Serpent says to Eve, "You see things, and you say 'Why?' But I dream things that never were; and I say 'Why not?'"[24] At approximately the same time as the events in Didion's novel are supposed to have transpired, Bobby Kennedy was adapting this passage from Shaw as a statement of political idealism. If we view Maria's "reply" to BZ as a profoundly pessimistic utterance, then the Kennedy allusion must be understood ironically. (Indeed, some would suggest that the optimism which Kennedy represented died with him where many of our

American dreams die—in California.) If, however, we concentrate only on the Shavian context, we might conclude that Maria's determination to accept life on its own hideous terms—in effect, to play it as it lays—is ultimately Satanic. The logical implication of her position is to reject the terms of Camus' dilemma. For Maria there are *no* significant philosophical problems.

In examining Didion's writings about the movie capital, we must finally wonder whether to give greater credence to the relatively sanguine view of that place articulated in her essays or to the nightmare vision of her Hollywood novel. To resolve this dilemma, however, we need to understand the difference between the author's respective approaches to journalism and to fiction. In her journalism she is trying to tell us what she knows about a particular subject (much as Alicia sought to tell the readers of the *Los Angeles Free Press* what she knew about the University of Michigan). But in her fiction Didion is trying to tell us the stories which certain mental images suggest to her. Let us, then, consider the image which served as the basis for *Play It as It Lays*.

In "Why I Write" Didion recalls having seen "a young woman with long hair and a short white halter dress . . . [walk] through the casino at the Riviera in Las Vegas at one in the morning. She crosses the casino alone and picks up a house telephone." The author watches this woman "because I have heard her paged, and recognize her name. . . . [But] I know nothing about her. Who is paging her? Why is she here to be paged? How exactly did she come to this?" "It was precisely this moment in Las Vegas," Didion concludes, "that made *Play It as It Lays* begin to tell itself to me" (p. 98).

It is important for us—as readers—to keep this image in mind, not only to see the young actress as Didion sees her, but also to see Didion looking *at* her. In short, to lose sight of the ironic perspective in this novel is inevitably to misread its author's intentions. At one level, Maria's story is one of genuine suffering and despair. Yet, at another level, Didion seems to be writing a parody of the novel of despair. She does this not by minimizing or ridiculing Maria's plight, but by undercutting the kinds of philosophical responses to that plight which romantic-existentialist writers might invoke.

Perhaps we can better understand Didion's attitude here if we consider the treatment of "nothingness"—or *nada*—in one of the most famous works of romantic-existentialist fiction: Ernest Hemingway's "A Clean, Well-Lighted Place." According to Carlos Baker, Hemingway's greatest achievement in this story lies in his "development, through the most carefully controlled understatement, of the young waiter's mere *nothing* into the old waiter's Something—a Something called Nothing which is so huge, terrible, overbearing, inevitable, and omnipresent that, once experienced, it can never be forgotten."[25] BZ and Maria have both experienced something very similar to the *nada* of Hemingway's story. BZ responds to that experience by allowing it to become for him a something called Nothing. Maria, however, is living testament to the fact that Nothing is—in fact—*no thing*.

No, Maria is not Prince Hamlet, nor was she meant to be. Neither is Hollywood—for Didion—Baudelaire's Unreal City. What we have in *Play It as It Lays* is a kind of postexistentialist nihilism which not only differs philosophically from the vision of a Hemingway or a Camus, but which also obviates the necessity of passing judgment on a region or an industry or—indeed—on anything at all. Nathanael West wrote about characters who packed up their shattered dreams and came west to die. Maria Wyeth, however, having pushed beyond the disillusionment which comes with shattered dreams, has come west to live. And that, in the still center of her daylight world, may well be a fate worse than death.

CHAPTER 10

The Witness I Wanted To Be

JOAN Didion's third novel, *A Book of Common Prayer*, is set in the imaginary Central American republic of Boca Grande; which is to say that the action of that novel transpires in a menacing social vacuum. (In the "Letters from Central America" which Didion's protagonist Charlotte tries unsuccessfully to sell to the *New Yorker* she refers to Boca Grande as a "land of contrasts"; however, Didion's narrator, Grace, informs us that this country is, in fact, "relentlessly the same," p. 13.)[1] Grace Strasser-Mendana, *née* Tabor, is our guide to Boca Grande as well as our witness to the life and death of Charlotte Douglas. Grace is a sixty-year-old anthropologist who has married into one of the nation's three or four solvent families. Her husband's death has left her "in putative control of fifty-nine-point eight percent of the arable land and about the same percentage of the decision-making process in Boca Grande" (pp. 18–19). And it is in Boca Grande that Grace meets Charlotte Douglas and begins to learn of her confused and pointless life.

Charlotte's story is a deceptively simple one: "she left one man, she left a second man, she traveled again with the first; she let him die alone. She lost one child to 'history' and another to 'complications' . . . , she imagined herself capable of shedding that baggage and came to Boca Grande, a tourist" (p. 11). Like so many of Didion's characters Charlotte is a westerner—from Hollister, California. She spends two years at Berkeley, where she meets and marries an untenured English instructor named Warren Bogart. Perversely charming and a bit sadistic, Warren is the first of the men whom Charlotte leaves. He is also the father of the child she loses to history.

Although she is only a minor character in her own right, that child—Marin Bogart—plays a significant role in her mother's story by deeply affecting Charlotte's psyche. Marin derives much of her credibility from the reader's assumed knowledge of radical youth politics of the late 1960s and early 1970s, particularly of the Patricia Hearst case.[2] Marin comes from a relatively conventional, upper-middle-class background and she appears to be a dull, unremarkable adolescent. At sixteen she "had been photographed with her two best friends wearing the pink-and-white candy-striped pinafores of Children's Hospital volunteers, and had later abandoned her Saturdays at the hospital as 'too sad'" (p. 58). But at eighteen this same child of the middle class "had been observed with her four best friends detonating a crude pipe bomb in the lobby of the Transamerica Building at 6:30 A.M., highjacking a P.S.A. L-1011 at San Francisco Airport and landing it at Wendover, Utah, where they burned it in time for the story to interrupt the network news and disappeared" (p. 58).

After Marin's disappearance Charlotte conceives another child, this time by her second husband—Leonard Douglas—a prominent San Francisco attorney who specializes in defending radical causes. She then leaves Leonard to return to Warren Bogart, and together she and Warren travel through the modern South, where they stay at a succession of cheap motels after wearing out their welcome with a host of Warren's friends and casual acquaintances. Charlotte finally leaves Warren a second time and returns to New Orleans, where she gives birth prematurely to a hydrocephalic child "devoid of viable liver function" (p. 147). The child dies in Yucatán and Charlotte flees aimlessly to Boca Grande, hoping someday to be reunited with Marin, for "in a certain dim way Charlotte believed that she had located herself at the very cervix of the world, the place through which a child lost to history must eventually pass" (p. 197).

While in Boca Grande Charlotte tries to live her life oblivious to the random political violence that surrounds her. But finally Charlotte Douglas is herself lost to history. She is shot in one of the periodic uprisings that constitute the only "history" that Boca Grande has ever known. Grace sees that Charlotte's body is placed in a coffin and is flown back to San Francisco. Since she is unable to find a flag with which to drape the coffin, Grace purchases a child's T-shirt which is printed like the American flag, but which lacks the correct number of stars and stripes. The novel closes with Grace pondering the enigma that was Charlotte Douglas, while awaiting her own imminent death by pancreatic cancer.

When a writer chooses a point of view for his narrative he is making an essentially epistemological decision. As Samuel Hynes points out, "a novel is a version of the ways in which a man can know reality, as well as a version of reality itself. The techniques by which a novelist controls our contact with his fictional world, and particularly his choice of point of view and his treatment of time, combine to create a model of a theory of knowledge."[3] In a sense the question of knowledge becomes more troublesome as our understanding of external reality becomes less certain. Although it may have been possible for Fielding and Dickens to preside over their respective fictional worlds with God-like certitude, the modern writer—living as he does in a more relativist universe—tends to be altogether more skeptical and more self-effacing. Novelists since Henry James have increasingly adopted a limited point of view.[4] And "when we speak of a limited-point-of-view novel," Hynes writes, "we are talking about a novel which implies a limited theory of knowledge" (p. 225). The point of view of Grace Strasser-Mendana is a veritable paradigm of such limitations.

Grace's understanding of Charlotte Douglas is limited by time and space, by human subjectivity, and by the arbitrary nature of language itself.[5] Indeed, far from trying to transcend these difficulties through rhetorical certitude or narrative sleight-of-hand, Didion makes them the focus of her novel. As critic John Romano writes:

Grace's own story is an allegory of the progress of the liberal, humanistic intelligence in the last twenty years. Out of a background informed by the fashionable cultural relativism of the 50's, through a disillusioning alliance with political power in the 60's, Grace emerges in the flat morning light of the present decade with . . . a will to plot the vagaries of the human individual on a graph of "significant" social and behavioral factors. . . . But the punchline is that Grace fails. The individual is at once bigger and more mysterious than the mechanistic models that are meant to comprehend her.[6]

Nor is Grace unaware of her failure. At the outset of the novel, after she has introduced herself to us, she says, "I tell you these things about myself only to legitimize my voice. We are uneasy about a story until we know who is telling it. In no other sense does it matter who 'I' am: 'the narrator' plays no motive role in this narrative, nor would I want to. . . . I am interested in Charlotte Douglas only insofar as she passed through Boca Grande, only insofar as the meaning of that sojourn continues to elude me" (p. 21). And at the end of the novel Grace's self-doubt is even more emphatic: "I am less and less certain that this story has been one of delusion," she says. "Unless the delusion was mine. . . . I have not been the witness I wanted to be" (p. 272). Like the Cretan poet Epimenides who declared that all Cretans were liars, Grace confronts us with a logical paradox. She is a narrator who frankly confesses her unreliability.

Grace's confession, however, is not the sort of aesthetic and rhetorical posturing that one might find in the more precious fiction of Barth or Barthelme. There is very little if any ironic distance between Didion as author and Grace as narrator. This is not to say that Grace is Didion's alter ego, but rather that Grace's intelligence, sympathy, and candor are characteristic of the author's own sensibility. It is hard to find a significant point in the novel where Grace's interpretation of events is clearly false or ludicrous. Her point of view may be limited, but so, too, is ours.

Formalistically, Grace represents what Robert Scholes and Robert Kellogg see as the "typical Conradian" narrator, a compromise between what one might call third-person-choric and first-person-protagonist narration. Such a narrator is an eyewitness who tells another person's story and who seeks to understand that person "through an imaginative sharing of his experience."[7] "This has been a very fruitful device in modern fiction," write Scholes and Kellogg. "The story of the protagonist becomes the outward sign or symbol of the inward story of the narrator, who learns from his imaginative participation in the other's experience. Since the imagination plays the central role, the factual or empirical aspect of the protagonist's life becomes subordinated to the narrator's understanding of it. Not what really happened but the meaning of what the narrator believes to have happened becomes the central preoccupation in this kind of narrative" (p. 261).

Examples of the peripheral narrator abound in modern American fiction. One thinks of Nick Carraway in *The Great Gatsby*, of Jack Burden in *All the King's Men*, and of Shreve and Quentin in *Absalom, Absalom!*[8] By dividing his narrator from his protagonist, the author obviates the "problem of presenting a character with enough crudeness for *hybris* and *hamartia* but enough sensitivity for ultimate discovery and self understanding" (Scholes and Kellogg, pp. 261–62).

In Charlotte Douglas, Didion gives us an unreflective protagonist, and in Grace Strasser-Mendana, the woman who chooses to be Charlotte's "witness," an intelligent and sensitive narrator. At one level, *A Book of Common Prayer* is the story of Charlotte's distress, of her inability to cope with the chaos of her life. In this sense she is not unlike Lily McClellan and Maria Wyeth. However, Didion's third novel is not simply a repetition of the themes of fragmentation and nothingness which we encounter in *Run River* and in *Play It as It Lays*. For Grace's narration is more functional, more genuinely symbolic, than are the points of view of Didion's first two novels. When asked about her technical intention for *A Book of Common Prayer* its author pointed to something she had written on a map of Central America: "Surface like rainbow slick, shifting, fall, thrown away, iridescent." "I wanted to do a deceptive surface," she said, "that appeared to be one thing and turned color as you looked through it" (Davidson interview, p. 36). The deceptive rainbow-slick surface of Didion's third novel is due in large part to the voice of her narrator.

But what of the novel's title? Why call this most secular of stories *A Book of Common Prayer*? Although the answer to such questions is hardly clear, one may venture tentative speculations. To begin with, it seems to me that the author of a first-person novel can make his presence known—independent of his narrator—only in a limited number of ways. He can do so ironically by using a *transparently* obtuse dramatic speaker (a tradition that goes back at least to the dramatic monologues of Browning) or he can follow the example of Eliot and employ a symbolically suggestive title and epigraph. Having foregone both an obtuse narrator[9] and any epigraph, Didion can intrude in her own person only by providing a suggestive title for her novel. This she has done with *A Book of Common Prayer*. At one point she told her editor, the late Henry Robbins, that her novel was actually Grace's prayer for Charlotte's soul. Although she admits to Sara Davidson that this explanation was "specious," Didion goes on to say, "If you have a narrator, which suddenly I was stuck with, the narrator can't just be telling you a story, something that happened, to entertain you. The narrator has got to be telling you the story for a reason. I think the title probably helped me with that" (p. 37).

The prose of *A Book of Common Prayer* does have a liturgical cadence. The repetition of key phrases and the frequent paragraph divisions give Didion's novel a sound and an appearance not unlike that of the Anglican prayer book. The real significance of Didion's title, however, is probably more thematic than formalistic. We know from her review of Cheever's *Falconer* that she considers her background as a white middle-class Episcopalian to be an important influence on her sensibility. Although Didion scarcely mentions religion in her novel, she does concern herself with the plight of characters who are *culturally* white, middle-class, and Protestant. (If Marin is sent to an Episcopal day school it is not because her mother is a devout Episcopalian, but because Charlotte is of a certain cultural heritage, because she is the inheritor of no dark or bloodied ground.)

The Anglican *Book of Common Prayer* is the oldest Protestant[10] liturgy in the English language. The services in that book fulfill the ancient function of ritual—they help give a certain order and coherence to our contemplation of spiritual things. (John Crowe Ransom argues that, since ritual is an essential component of human life, it is necessary for one to retain a *sense* of ritual even after he has ceased to believe in religious dogma.[11] Accordingly, Didion admits that though she no longer goes to church, she frequently repeats phrases from the prayer book in her mind [Davidson interview, p. 38].) What its author has given us in *A Book of Common Prayer* is Grace's attempt to find some sense of order and coherence in the life of Charlotte Douglas. Grace is "witnessing" for Charlotte in much the same way that a believer might witness for his faith. The salient difference, of course, is that Grace has not found order and coherence in Charlotte's life, only chaos and fragmentation; she has not come to rest in a sure faith, but remains a confirmed skeptic. She has been able only to shore some fragments against her ruin.[12] And the most grotesque irony of all is that hers is quite literally the ruin of Grace.[13] Hers is a death by cancer.

Una Turista

At one level Charlotte Douglas's story is one of classic American innocence. She is not the sort of naive but triumphant American whom Henry James used to send to Europe,[14] nor is she exactly like the self-conscious expatriates of Hemingway. Instead, she is "a suffering heroine for whom we feel more compassion than she is capable of feeling for herself— . . . [one who] embodies Kierkegaard's unnerving paradox that a person can be in despair and not know it" (Romano, p. 63). She is a child of the American West.

As a child of comfortable family in the temperate zone . . . [Charlotte] had been as a matter of course provided with clean sheets, orthodontia, lamb chops, living grandparents, attentive godparents, one brother named Dickie, ballet lessons, and casual timely information about menstruation and the care of flat silver. . . . She had been provided as well with faith in the value of certain frontiers on which her family had lived, in the virtues of cleared and irrigated land, of high yield crops, of thrift, industry and the judicial system, of progress and education, and in the generally upward spiral of history. (pp. 59–60)

Charlotte is an impulsive, unreflective person. (Grace says of her: "I think I have never known anyone who led quite so unexamined a life" [p. 112].) At a picnic given for working-class children in Boca Grande, she grabs a chicken on the run and snaps the vertebrae in its neck. The men at the picnic "were killing chickens with machetes but Charlotte's kill was clean" (p. 49). And later Grace tells us that she once saw Charlotte "make the necessary incision in the trachea of an OAS field worker who was choking on a piece of steak at the Jockey Club. A doctor had been called but the OAS man was turning blue.

Charlotte did it with a boning knife plunged first in a vat of boiling rice." "A few nights later," however, "the OAS man caused a scene because Charlotte refused to fellate him on the Caribe terrace." This scene, Grace tells us, was "suggestive of the ambiguous signals Charlotte tended to transmit" (p. 61).

Charlotte's attitude toward sex is consistent with the rest of her outlook on life. Hers is an innocence which has nothing to do with chastity. Rather, her idealism and her simplicity leave her peculiarly defenseless in a world that is often cynical and hideously complex. "I think I have never known anyone," Grace says, "who regarded the sexual connection as quite so unamusing a contract":

> So dark and febrile and outside the range of the normal did all aspects of this contract seem to Charlotte that she was for example incapable of walking normally across a room in the presence of two men with whom she had slept. Her legs seemed to lock unnaturally into her pelvic bones. Her body went stiff, as if convulsed by the question of who had access to it and who did not. . . . I recall once telling Charlotte about a village on the Orinoco where female children were ritually cut on the inner thigh by their first sexual partners, the point being to scar the female with the male's totem. Charlotte saw nothing extraordinary in this. "I mean that's pretty much what happens everywhere isn't it," she said. "Somebody cuts you? Where it doesn't show?" (p. 85)

Like Maria Wyeth and so many other moderns, Charlotte suffers from temporal provincialism. She is inclined instinctively to "avoid the backward glance." And "until Marin disappeared Charlotte had arranged her days to do exactly that" (p. 96). However, after Marin takes her mother's hopes for the future with her, Charlotte tries desperately to recover some sense of her past. Haunted by memories of the chicken à la king and overdone biscuits her grandmother used to cook, Charlotte returns to the family ranch in Hollister, now occupied by her brother Dickie and his wife, Linda. The experience proves even less rewarding than do Maria's encounters with Benny Austin.

To begin with, Linda is overtly hostile to Charlotte. She manages to dispatch her children to the local gym—after a dinner of Kraft macaroni and cheese—for the entirety of Charlotte's visit. Linda exudes a clean-living shrewishness that is calculated to insult Charlotte, while Dickie sulks, drinks, and bemoans the sexual poverty of his marriage. Apparently Warren had preceded Charlotte's visit to the ranch with one of his own. He had stayed for eleven hours and a quart and a half of expensive gin and he had been accompanied by an old friend—a Negro bartender from the Roosevelt Hotel in New Orleans. Clearly, Linda was not amused.

At the end of dinner Charlotte asks Dickie if he remembers their grandmother's biscuits and he responds in nonsequitur fashion by telling Charlotte that the ranch is the only home she has ever had:

> "Oh, fine," Linda said. "Back to Tara. The Havemeyers are off to the races now. If you're looking for your car keys they're on the coffee table. Next to the ring from Massa Richard's glass."
>
> "Remember the biscuits, Dickie? Halfway through dinner we'd smell them burning?"
>
> "The only thing I remember your famous grandmother burning is every bedjacket I ever took her in the nursing home." Linda handed Charlotte her car keys.
>
> "Smoking in bed. Little holes in every one." (pp. 134–35)

As his sister leaves Dickie says, "'You and me, Char.'" He "touched Charlotte's hair uncertainly and turned away. 'Forget goddamn Marin. I say give her a Kraft Dinner and I say the hell with her'" (p. 135).

By most objective standards Charlotte's life with Leonard Douglas would seem to be reasonably happy. Leonard is successful, even-tempered, and genuinely interested in his wife's welfare. Warren Bogart, on the other hand, is none of these things. Nevertheless, Leonard is perhaps too decent, too rational, and too liberal ever to satisfy the self-martyred romantic in Charlotte. Although Didion tries hard not to caricature Leonard, he strikes one as being fairly typical of a certain "radical chic" sensibility. He has been in analysis for eight years and his psychiatrist, Polly Orben, "frequently reported that they were within a year or so of 'terminating' or 'ending'" (p. 71). He even keeps marijuana in a silver music box that plays "Puff the Magic Dragon." According to Warren, Leonard and Charlotte do not have a life together; they have a "life-style" (p. 110).

For reasons that are not made altogether clear, Charlotte abandons this "life-style" to return to Warren.[15] He apparently possesses for her a demonic appeal not unlike that displayed by Ryder Channing in *Run River* and Carter Lang in *Play It as It Lays*. Yet Warren is a much more fully realized character than either Ryder or Carter. His personality is so vivid, in fact, that Warren tends to dominate every scene that he is in. We may not understand Charlotte's attraction to Warren, but he is a thoroughly believeable scoundrel: "Like many Southerners and like some Catholics and unlike Charlotte he was raised to believe not in 'hard work' or 'self-reliance' but in the infinite power of the personal appeal, the request for a favor, the intervention of one or another merciful Virgin. He had an inchoate but definite conviction that access to the mysteries of good fortune was arranged in the same way as access to the Boston Club, a New Orleans institution to which he did not belong but always had a guest card" (pp. 162–63).[16]

(Charlotte's life with Warren begins in a way which prefigures their future sadomasochistic relationship. At the age of nineteen she writes a paper on Melville for Warren's class and he fails her on it. He then shows up at her apartment at midnight with Charlotte's paper torn in half and with a faintly Dionysian bag of cherries and a bottle of bourbon. They stay at her place for forty-eight hours and then Warren takes Charlotte to his apartment and asks her to clean it up. There she comes across a letter from his department chairman advising Warren that his contract will not be renewed.)

When Charlotte leaves Leonard Douglas she and Warren head south, ostensibly to visit a dying relative who has played sugar daddy to many of Warren's ill-fated business and cultural ventures. As it turns out that relative is, in fact, not dying, but Warren is. He spends his last months drinking himself senseless, abusing Charlotte, and generally annoying everyone with whom he comes into contact. What makes Warren positively appealing, however, is his sheer verbal brilliance. (To find an equally literate quality of malice in modern American writing, one would need to turn to Edward Albee's *Who's Afraid of Virginia Woolf?* But unlike Albee's characters, Warren has no rival among his peers for either wit or venom. His victims are frequently passive and almost always inarticulate.)

Warren is at his obnoxious best on the one occasion in which Grace encounters him. Several months after Charlotte's arrival in Boca Grande, Grace leaves for New Orleans to receive cobalt treatments and to renegotiate some copra contracts. She is at the Garden District home of a friend when Warren arrives, uninvited, with a young lady of almost catatonic servility. Warren gleefully ignores every hint that he should leave, brings up subjects that are sure to cause domestic strife, and forces his date to recite such memorable anthology pieces as "Crossing the Bar," "Thanatopsis," and "Snowbound." "'Do "Snowbound,"' Warren Bogart said. 'There's nobody here wouldn't be improved by hearing "Snowbound"'" (p. 168).

The South through which Warren and Charlotte travel is not the South of William Faulkner or of Eudora Welty. Rather it is the Sunbelt South of Walker Percy. The gentility and graciousness which were once thought characteristic of the South have degenerated into such transparently forced civility that one of her "hosts" can say to Charlotte, "The idea, your friend Warren going off and leaving you here alone, might not matter to you but it matters to me, a man insults a lady in my house and he insults me. You wouldn't understand that, Mrs. Douglas, I'm certain it's all free and easy where your people come from" (p. 180).

One suspects that the reason Warren enjoys traveling in the South is that southerners are more easily offended than are the cosmopolitan inhabitants of Leonard Douglas's world. ("His favorite hand was outrageousness," Grace tells us; "in a fluid world like Leonard Douglas's where no one could be outraged Warren Bogart was dimmed, confused, unable to operate" [p. 162]). When Charlotte complains to Warren about the treatment they have received, he accuses her of being insufficiently familiar with "normal people," of being too used to Arabs and Jews. And Charlotte replies, "I can't help noticing Arabs and Jews are rather less insulting to their houseguests." "Not to this houseguest they wouldn't be, babe," Warren responds. "You show me an Arab who'll put up with me, I'll show you an Arab who doesn't get the picture" (pp. 180–81).

In distinguishing between "normal people," on the one hand, and "Arabs and Jews," on the other, Warren—like John McClellan in *Run River*—deals less in facts than in social attitudes. "Normal people" are, by definition, those who respond to Warren in a particular way. (We are told that such people can be found not only in the South, but also in academia and on the Upper East Side of New York.) For "normal people," Warren is a charming boor, a witty iconoclast whom they love to hate. (They see him as an updated version of Alexander Woolcott[17] with a bit of the Marquis de Sade thrown in for good measure.) However, for "Arabs and Jews" (that is, contemporary jet-setters) he is simply a tired, irrelevant anachronism. They "put up" with him by ignoring him. And to someone of Warren Bogart's sensibility, such tolerance is the unkindest slight of all.

The various stops which Warren and Charlotte make on their southern odyssey are not clearly distinguished one from another. Instead, that odyssey is rendered impressionistically: one remembers only disjointed scenes and phrases, the feeling of pain inflicted and of pain received, and a sense of diurnal chaos:

She was a woman almost forty whose fillings hurt when the highway vibrated. She was a woman almost forty waiting for the night when she would call to get the Demerol. When Warren woke at sundown he took her to see a bike movie in a drive-in and drank a fifth of bourbon in the car and drove under the big pink arc lights with the rented car flat-out all the way to Birmingham. When the peonies swelled and broke behind her eyelids in the Ochsner Clinic they blazed like the big pink arc lights all the way to Birmingham. She could take care of somebody or somebody could take care of her and it was the same thing in the end. (p. 189)

If, as Joyce Carol Oates contends, "Joan Didion has never been easy on her heroines" (p. 34), she has been positively brutal to the babies in her novels. Lily McClellan and Maria Wyeth both have abortions and Charlotte Douglas gives birth to a deformed child. In each novel, however, the mother-infant relationship is somewhat fuller than in the preceding one. Although Lily thinks of herself as only terminating a pregnancy, Maria realizes that she is killing an unborn child. And Charlotte, in contrast to the other two mothers, goes to heroic lengths to care for her baby. In characteristic fashion, Leonard argues against her even seeing the child, while Warren tries to torment Charlotte during the vulnerable days of her recovery from giving birth.

Charlotte leaves New Orleans and takes her baby with her to Yucatán, thinking that it will die more quickly there. But the child takes a long time to die and the descriptions of its dying are almost too painful to read. At least Charlotte has made sure that she is there when the end comes:

The baby did not die at the Mérida airport but an hour later, in the parking lot of the Coca-Cola bottling plant on the road back into town. The baby had gone into convulsions and projectile vomiting in the taxi and Charlotte had made the driver stop in the parking lot. She walked with the baby on the dark asphalt. She sang to the baby out on the edge of the asphalt where the rushes grew and a few trailers were parked. By the time the baby died the taxi had left but it was only a mile or two to the Centro Médico de Yucatán and Charlotte walked there with the baby in her arms, trusting at last, its vomit spent. (p. 150)

After her child is buried Charlotte returns to the cemetery and tries unsuccessfully to find the baby's grave. "It was not a large cemetery but there seemed a large number of small fresh unmarked graves. She left the bougainvillea she had torn from the wall of the hotel on one of them" (p. 152).

Charlotte's "normal" child—Marin—is her mother's chief obsession in life. Grace tells us that when Charlotte died "she cried not for God but for Marin" (p. 268). (Here again, we see a progression through Didion's first three novels. Although Marin remains a somewhat vague presence, her character is more fully developed than that of either Julie McClellan or Kate Lang. All we know of Julie is that she swims naked and lusts for a T-Bird with a stick shift, while Kate is mentally retarded.) It seems to me that Charlotte—like Maria Wyeth—builds her hopes for the future on a child who is incapable of being reached. Because Marin does not suffer from the same sort of neurological disorder which afflicts Kate, she would appear to be potentially more accessible to Charlotte than Kate is to Maria. Ultimately, though, Marin lacks the intelligence and the character necessary to deal with the world around her, much less to forge a lasting bond with her mother.[18] Perhaps Warren sums up his daughter's personality most succinctly. "Marin can't read," he says. "She plays a good game of tennis, she's got a nice backhand, good strong hair and an IQ of about 103" (p. 99).

Although Marin's is the most inherently melodramatic story in the novel, it is one which we know only through indirection. For the most part, we do not witness Marin herself, but rather Marin's effect on Charlotte (or, to put the matter more precisely, Grace's interpretation of Marin's effect on Charlotte).[19] We get our first sense of what this effect might be when Charlotte tells Grace of a trip which she and her daughter had taken to the Tivoli Gardens in Copenhagen.

The colored lights strung outside the Capilla del Mar in Boca Grande remind Charlotte of Tivoli. She and Marin had flown there one weekend and they had seen the puppet shows and the watermills. "They had made dinners of salami and petits fours. They had scarcely slept. They had wandered beneath the colored lights until Marin's heels blistered, and then they had taken off their shoes and wandered barefoot" (p. 47). Finally, mother and daughter had returned to the hotel room and had ordered cocoa from room service. "And I let Marin place the order and tip the waiter," Charlotte says. "And I taught her how to wash out her underwear at night" (p. 47). Two weeks after telling this story to Grace, Charlotte mentions that during her trip to Tivoli Marin had run a fever in reaction to her smallpox vaccination. They had had to stay in their hotel room. And it had rained all weekend anyway. Just as Maria—at the end of *Play It as It Lays*—imagines a pastoral future with Kate, so too does Charlotte manufacture an idyllic past with Marin.

Marin appears in the novel in only one brief scene, which is itself divided between chapters forty-four pages apart (pp. 213–14, 258–60). Otherwise, our perception of her is based on decidedly peripheral evidence. For example, the tape she releases—à la Patty Hearst—is a brilliant parody of revolutionary rhetoric. *"The fact that our organization is revolutionary in character,"* she declares in utter seriousness, *"is due above all to the fact that all our activity is defined as revolutionary"* (p. 82). The description of her room in Leonard's house also reveals much about Marin's personality: "After the FBI men left that morning Charlotte went upstairs to Marin's room. The Raggedy Ann Warren had sent for Marin's twelfth birthday was on its shelf. The teddy bear Warren had sent for Marin's fourteenth Easter was on its chair. The guitar once used by Joan Baez was on the windowseat, where it had been since the night Leonard bought it for Marin at an ACLU auction. . . . All that Marin had removed from the room was every picture, every snapshot, every clipping or class photograph, which contained her own image" (p. 67). Although that image eventually appears on network news broadcasts and in post offices across the nation, "Charlotte always referred to the day Marin hijacked the L-1011 and burned it on the Bonneville Salt Flats as 'when Marin went to Utah,' as if it had been a tour of National Parks" (pp. 239–40).

In her lone appearance in the novel Marin seems mostly wooden and two-dimensional. (Although such an effect may be intended, Didion comes perilously close here to committing the fallacy of imitative form.) We do get a glimpse through Marin's vacuous exterior, however, in a moment of revelation which suggests much while saying little. When she locates Charlotte's daughter in a tenement apartment in Buffalo, Grace asks Marin how she liked the Tivoli Gardens. As she moves away from the refrigerator to fix Grace some ice water, Marin splashes water from the ice tray onto the floor, and she explodes: "God*damn* people around here, somebody took it out last night and never put it back, I mean *I* had to put it back this morning, I don't think—" (p. 260). She continues in this vein until Grace repeats the word "Tivoli." Marin then breaks down "exactly as her mother must have broken the morning the FBI first came to the house on California Street" (p. 260). Although this scene sheds no light on Tivoli, it suggests a good deal about the enigmatic relationship between Charlotte Douglas and the daughter she loses to history.

The theme of maternity also comes up in contexts that are not directly related to Charlotte and Marin. In each case we see a distortion or an attenuation of the traditional family structure. Early in the novel, for example, Grace indicates that her son Gerardo is as lost to her as Marin is to Charlotte. Gerardo even refers to his mother by her first name, as if to suggest that the conventional mother-child relationship no longer obtains. Another commentary on family structure occurs at a party which Charlotte attends shortly after Marin's disappearance. Here an actress who had recently visited Hanoi speaks of "the superior health and beauty of the children there." "'It's because they aren't raised by their mothers,' the actress said. 'They don't have any of that bourgeois personal crap laid on them. . . . No mama-papa-baby-nuclear-family bullshit. . . . It's beautiful'" (p. 130). In the colloquial, non-Aristotelian sense of the term, Joan Didion's first three novels are all domestic tragedies. The family may well be the last institution standing between the individual and the abyss, the last of what sociologists call "mediating structures." If so, the breakdown of the family becomes a kind of synecdoche for the fragmentation of our entire culture.

Superficially, it would seem appropriate that Charlotte, who is called the "*norteamericana* cunt," should spend her final days in Boca Grande, "the cervix of the world." For Charlotte is a woman who avoids the backward glance and Boca Grande is a country without history. ("Every time the sun falls on a day in Boca Grande that day appears to vanish from local memory, to be reinvented if necessary but never recalled" [p. 14].) However, by the end of the novel we realize that Charlotte's virtually Adamic innocence,[20] which accounts for her avoidance of history, is nothing short of disastrous in the perverse and cynical environment of Boca Grande. As an optimistic child of the western United States, she is actually out of place in a land which lacks a future as well as a past, a land where all time is frozen in a present "relentlessly the same."

A prime example of Charlotte's North American innocence can be found in her absurdly ingenuous display of compassion toward some children in Boca Grande. She notices that every morning three small children climb under the fence surrounding the swimming pool at the Caribe Hotel. Although they apparently do not know how to swim, the children leap into the deep end of the pool and flounder and gasp from one side to the other. "There was no lifeguard and the water was green with algae and Charlotte could never see the children beneath the surface of the water but every morning she would take her breakfast to the pool and try to insure that the children did not drown" (p. 228). The manager of the Caribe refuses to take any action because there are no children registered at the hotel. Then one morning when she can see only two of the three children for thirty straight seconds Charlotte jumps into the pool, fully clothed and screaming. "She choked and the murky water blinded her and when she came up all three children were standing on the edge of the pool fighting over her handbag" (p. 229). In a way these urchins are older than Charlotte will ever be.

If it is not altogether clear why Charlotte has come to Boca Grande, it is even less clear why she stays. At one level her insistence on remaining may simply be another indication of her solipsistic innocence. Despite sufficient warning, she chooses to ignore the danger that surrounds her. When a bomb goes off in the clinic where she works, Charlotte remembers only that she bled (not from any wounds, but because she was changing a Tampax at the time). In a larger sense, though, her decision to stay in Boca Grande is a gratuitous act of courage. She says to Leonard, *"I walked away from places all my life and I'm not going to walk away from here"* (p. 256). Charlotte's death accomplishes nothing tangible, but in an absurd world one can do no more than make an existential gesture. (The doomed characters in *Play It as It Lays* cannot even do that.) And so *A Book of Common Prayer* is at least marginally affirmative, for in restoring some nobility to death Joan Didion suggests that life itself may not be utterly devoid of meaning.

CHAPTER 11

"Threescore Miles and Ten"

TOWARD the end of James Joyce's "The Dead" Gabriel Conroy stands at the foot of the stairs in his aunts' house and gazes up at his wife, Gretta. "There was grace and mystery in her attitude as if she were a symbol of something. He asked himself what is a woman standing on the stairs in the shadow, listening to distant music, a symbol of. If he were a painter he would paint her in that attitude. Her blue felt hat would show off the bronze of her hair against the darkness and the dark panels of her skirt would show off the light ones. *Distant Music* he would call the picture if he were a painter."[1]

I am reminded of this scene from Joyce whenever I think of Joan Didion's fiction. Like Gabriel, Didion's characters try to reshape reality, to make it "as finished and as self-contained as a painting on a gallery wall."[2] And even though their failure to do so is a foregone conclusion, one can infer much about Didion's fictional world by examining the ways in which her characters attempt to create fictions of their own. Charlotte Douglas, Maria Wyeth, and Mary Monroe Sweet, for example, imagine themselves to be ideal mothers (Charlotte has "Tivoli"; Maria her "house by the sea"; and Mary her baby food ad). Other characters in other works define themselves in terms of equally obsessive images: the unnamed protagonist of "When Did Music Come This Way . . . ?" believes that things were better during those childhood Christmases before 1945; Louisa Patterson Pool finds temporary solace in memories of "the apparently golden girl she had been" (p. 83);[3] and Lily McClellan feels that her very identity was buried in the family graveyard with her father. Because each of these characters is trapped in the present, each seeks escape: some through unrealistic hopes for the future, others through idealized recollections of the past.

(We might note in passing that Didion makes very literal use of "distant music" in her fictions. When we think of her stories we think of the songs which Mary Monroe Sweet's father composed about his daughter on the Chickering, of the broken music box in "When Did Music Come This Way . . . ?" and of the world of Louisa Pool's adolescence where "'Blue Moon' segued incessantly into 'Heart and Soul'" [p. 33]. And even in her novels—where it sounds much less insistently than in her stories—the strains of distant music can still be heard. Lily, for example, hums a few bars of "Blue Room" as her marriage disintegrates around her;[4] Maria fondly recalls her mother's crooning: *"cross the ocean in a plane . . . see the jungle when it's wet with rain"* [p. 7]; and one night in Boca Grande Charlotte stays up until three A.M., seated at a ballroom piano, "picking out with one hand, over and over again and in every possible tempo, the melodic line of a single song . . . 'Mountain Greenery'" [p. 24].[5])

Of course, as we recall from the discussion of cracked crab and August snow in her essay "On Keeping a Notebook," Didion is herself familiar with the impulse to remember events less as they were than as they ought to have been. Yet, because she has the advantage of realizing what she is doing, her sense of self-awareness enables her to avoid the pitfalls of solipsism. Such self-awareness is evident in a passage from "In Praise of Unhung Wreaths and Love." Here, she "remembers" the California Christmases of her childhood when it would rain "a hard cold rain that darkened the sky at 4 o'clock and threatened the levees and provided a table topic." "It seems to me now that those Christmas afternoons in the rain were somehow 'better' than any since," she writes, "but of course I am lying to myself. Then as now, mothers and daughters misunderstood each other. Fathers and sons did not speak. I remember my mother telling me, after such an afternoon some years ago that Christmas used to be 'better,' that lately we all drank too much and gave one another too many presents."

This tendency to retreat into a rich imaginative life is no doubt exacerbated by the spiritual poverty of our public lives. Yet Didion is not alone in telling us that that sense of personal and social order which is the center of human continuity has failed to hold. Nor is she alone in telling us that when that center goes, some will respond with an autistic distrust of the external world. (Although Didion's characters have only a very tenuous hold on reality, none goes to the pathological extremes of, say, J. Henry Waugh in Robert Coover's *The Universal Baseball Association*.) No, we do not go to Didion primarily for a diagnosis of what is wrong with society: her analysis—though brilliantly realized—is hardly original. Neither do we go to her for "answers," for she has none. Instead, we find in her work a quality which her old teacher Mark Schorer calls "a triumph not of insight as such but of style."[6] When reading *Play It as It Lays* Schorer notes: "one thinks of the great *performers* in ballet, opera, circuses." This is not to say that Didion's craft is in any way pyrotechnical, but rather to agree with Alfred Kazin that her work commands our attention because of "the graphic readability it makes of our condition."[7]

Perhaps in a world where the substance of things is so nebulous, we are ultimately forced to "fall back on style" (a stance which BZ accuses Maria of taking when she describes his suicide as "a queen's way of doing it" [p. 212]). Didion's style, however, is informed by a moral seriousness which prevents it from degenerating into mere gimmickry. I suspect that those of us who find power and beauty in her work share the feeling which D. A. N. Jones experienced upon reading *Play It as It Lays*: of "a certain exhiliration, as when we appreciate a harmonious and well-proportioned painting of some cruelly martyred saint in whom we do not believe."[8]

It is too early to assess Joan Didion's place in American literature and it would be problematical to try to predict the future course of her career. At present, however, she has established herself as being—at the very least—a "writer's writer." Her most enthusiastic admirers include other talented literary artists, figures as diverse as Guy Davenport and Joyce Carol Oates, as Brian Moore and Tennessee Williams. Indeed, no less an authority than James Dickey has called her "the finest woman prose stylist writing in English today."[9]

In contrast, critics generally have been more hesitant and more reserved in their praise. *Run River* was virtually ignored in this country—though it did receive a favorable notice in the *Times Literary Supplement*—and *Play It as It Lays* was greeted with mixed reviews. (Ironically, some critics faulted the latter novel for being *too* well-written. "Her prose," one reviewer claims of Didion, "tends to posture like a figure from a decadent period of art, whose fingers curl toward an exposed heart or a draped bosom swelling with suspect emotion."[10]) Not until *A Book of Common Prayer* was she widely recognized as a major American novelist.

However, during those years in which she was attempting to establish her place in contemporary fiction, Didion was consistently praised for her journalistic efforts. Indeed, some critics have even suggested that she give up fiction altogether and focus exclusively on expository prose. Yet it appears unlikely that she will heed their advice (at the time of her interview with Sara Davidson she was working on both a novel and a nonfiction book). Nor should she. It probably would be a dissipation of talent for her to submit herself indefinitely to the demands of a regular column (just as it would be a waste of time for her to devote too much effort to the collaborative medium of screenwriting).

An area of journalism which might present Didion with an interesting literary challenge, though, is that of the "non-fiction novel"; for her achievement in "Some Dreamers of the Golden Dream" includes a skillful handling of nonfiction narrative and her use of political themes in *A Book of Common Prayer* suggests that she knows something about "the novel as history."[11] At one time she did consider writing a book based on tapes she made with and about Linda Kasabian, but that project has since been abandoned.

Nevertheless, fiction is still the higher dream, and it is here where we have the right to expect most of Didion. It is even conceivable that she will write a Western epic and thereby fulfill her promise as the California Faulkner. But if she is to do so, she must first learn how to deal with Snopeses as well as Sartorises. (Thus far, her fictional treatment of lower- and working-class people has been confined to amusing burlesque and to cloying condescension.[12]) Still, it would be a mistake to limit our expectations of her too quickly. Her talent is large and it seems capable of further growth. To see that this is so we need only remember that, prior to *A Book of Common Prayer*, she was judged incapable of creating believable, three-dimensional male characters; and then in the figure of Warren Bogart she gave us one of the most hauntingly memorable men in recent American fiction.

When Joan Didion turns on her china night lamp we see different pictures at different times shining through those translucent porcelain sides. We see the faint glimmer of the headlights of Walter Knight's car from beneath the surface of the river which took both his life and that of Martha McClellan; we see, in the perpetual light of Vegas, a young actress with long hair and a short white halter dress walking through a casino alone after midnight; and—yes—we see Charlotte and Warren, under big pink arc lights which shine like the breaking of peonies, as they drive flat-out in the rented car all the way to Birmingham. These images and dozens like them stay with us and live indelibly in the imagination. Their impact is not unlike the memory many years later of a childhood summer spent in Vermont, when the ground hardened one night and snow covered the face of an August morning.

Notes and References

Chapter One

1. She continues: "I remember learning more about orange spoons than about sin from the Episcopal Church, in which I was christened and confirmed (and in which I was told, when I said I feared death, that there was no hell; 'only different levels of heaven')." She "learned even less from the Catholic Church in which I was married (the boundary between mortal and venial sin, I was told when I expressed concern, 'differs from parish to parish')." See "The Way We Live Now," *National Review*, March 24, 1964, p. 237.

2. "Place in Fiction," in *The Eye of the Story* (New York, 1978), pp. 119–20.

3. *Slouching Towards Bethlehem* (New York, 1968). Page references in text; hereinafter referred to as *Slouching*.

4. *National Review*, March 25, 1961, pp. 190–91.

5. See Alfred Kazin, "Joan Didion: Portrait of a Professional," *Harper's*, December 1971, p. 112.

6. "American Summer," *Vogue*, May 1963, p. 117. Elsewhere, we read that one summer when she was in the eighth grade and romantically enthralled with the idea of death by drowning, "Joan determined to find out for herself how it would feel to walk into the ocean."

After telling her parents she and her brother, Jimmy, were going to a square dance, she dropped Jimmy off at the Greyhound bus terminal, told him to wait for her and went on to the shore herself. Then, note pad in hand, she gingerly walked into the ocean. The night was dark, and she had no sooner waded in knee-deep than a wave hit her in the face. Sopping wet, her romantic notions of suicide considerably dampened, she made her way back to the terminal, retrieved her brother, and sneaked back into the house.

See Michiko Kakutani, "Joan Didion: Staking Out California," *New York Times Magazine*, June 10, 1979, p. 40.

7. For a fuller discussion of Didion's essay comparing the old and new California governor's mansions, see Chapter 6 below.

8. All references are to p. 18. Close readers of Didion's fiction will recall that both Lily Knight and Marin Bogart attend Berkeley after being turned down by Stanford.

9. *The White Album* (New York, 1979). Page references in text; hereinafter referred to as *Album*.

10. In recalling the years she spent writing captions and advertising copy for that magazine, Didion observes: "It was at *Vogue* that I learned a kind of

ease with words . . . , a way of regarding words not as mirrors of my own inadequacy but as tools, toys, weapons to be deployed strategically on a page. . . . Less was more, smooth was better, and absolute precision essential to the monthly grand illusion. Going to work for *Vogue* was, in the late nineteen-fifties, not unlike training with the Rockettes." See Didion's *Telling Stories* (Berkeley, California, 1978), p. 5.

11. For an amusing account of this experience, see Didion's "When It Was Magic Time in Jersey," *Vogue*, September 15, 1962, pp. 33–35, 81.

12. "He and Joan met in New York on opposite halves of a double date. When John's girl passed out drunk in Didion's apartment, she fixed him red beans and rice and, he recalls, 'We talked all night.' Yet they remained only friends for six years until 1963, when they lunched to discuss the manuscript of her first novel *Run River*. A year later they married." See John Riley, "Couples: Writers Joan Didion and John Gregory Dunne Play It as It Lays in Malibu," *People*, July 26, 1976, p. 52.

13. *Oxford Dictionary of Nursery Rhymes* (London, 1951), p. 65.

14. For a more complete discussion of this adoption, see John Gregory Dunne, "Quintana," in *Quintana and Friends* (New York, 1978), pp. 3–9. Also, Dunne's *Vegas: Memoir of a Dark Season* (New York, 1974) provides additional insight into his marriage to Didion.

15. All references are to p. 34. (A revised version of this essay appears as part of a larger section of *The White Album*, pp. 133–36.) This particular exchange crops up in a conversation between Maria and BZ in the film version of *Play It as It Lays*.

16. See *Life*, December 19, 1969, p. 19.

17. She has, for example, suffered a series of visual disturbances caused by a neurological condition diagnosed as multiple sclerosis. Didion describes her response to this diagnosis as follows: "In a few lines of dialogue in a neurologist's office in Beverly Hills, the improbable had become probable, the norm: things which happened only to other people could in fact happen to me. I could be struck by lightning, could dare to eat a peach and be poisoned by the cyanide in the stone. The startling fact was this: my body was offering a precise physiological equivalent to what had been going on in my mind" (*Album*, p. 47).

18. See "Jealousy: Is It a Curable Illness?" *Vogue*, June 1961, p. 97.

19. All references are to p. 22.

20. All references are to p. 2B.

21. See Susan Braudy, "A Day in the Life of Joan Didion," *Ms.*, February 1977, p. 66. For a more detailed account of the Dunnes' work on *A Star Is Born*, see "Gone Hollywood," in *Quintana and Friends*, pp. 158–63.

22. See Beverly Gary Kempton, "He/She," *Self*, February 1979, pp. 36–38. In this interview Mr. and Mrs. Dunne discuss their rearing of Quintana according to Spock.

Chapter Two

1. *New York Times Book Review*, December 5, 1976, p. 2.

2. There is an even closer parallel between Didion's mode of composition and the one which Faulkner employed in writing *The Sound and the Fury.* Speaking of that novel, Faulkner says:

It began with a mental picture. I didn't realize at the time it was symbolical. The picture was of the muddy seat of a little girl's drawers in a pear tree, where she could see through a window where her grandmother's funeral was taking place and report what was happening to her brothers on the ground below. By the time I explained who they were and what they were doing and how her pants got muddy, I realized it would be impossible to get all of it into a short story and that it would have to be a book. And then I realized the symbolism of the soiled pants, and that image was replaced by one of the fatherless and motherless girl climbing down the rainpipe to escape from the only home she had, where she had never been offered love or affection or understanding.

See *Twentieth Century Interpretations of The Sound and the Fury,* ed. Michael H. Cowan (Englewood Cliffs, New Jersey, 1968), p. 16.

3. "Marks of Identity," *National Review,* March 25, 1961, p. 190.

4. "Finally (Fashionably) Spurious," *National Review,* November 18, 1961, p. 342.

5. See *Open Secrets: Ninety-four Women in Touch with Our Time,* ed. Barbaralee Diamonstein (New York, 1970), p. 104. For a fuller exposition of Didion's views on Elizabeth Hardwick, see her review of Hardwick's *Sleepless Nights* in *New York Times Book Review,* April 29, 1979, pp. 1, 60.

6. See Sara Davidson, "A Visit with Joan Didion," *New York Times Book Review,* April 3, 1977, p. 38. On that same page Didion also mentions Conrad, James and Hemingway as important early influences on her style.

7. In his review of *Slouching Towards Bethlehem (New York Times Book Review,* July 21, 1968, p. 8), Dan Wakefield applies this phrase of Didion's to her own work.

Chapter Three

1. *New York Times Book Review,* March 6, 1977, p. 1.

2. Although she cast her ballot for Goldwater in 1964, Didion has voted only twice since then. See Kakutani, p. 38.

3. All references are to p. 20. A revised version of this essay and of "The Revolution Game" appear as part of "The White Album."

4. All references are to p. 20.

5. Braudy, p. 66. For more extended feminist critiques of "The Women's Movement," see Judith Newton, "Joan Didion, 1972," in *Female Studies VI: Closer to the Ground,* eds. Nancy Hoffman, Cynthia Secor, and Adrian Tinsley (Old Westbury, New York, 1973), pp. 110–15; and Catherine Stimpson, "The Case of Miss Joan Didion," *Ms.,* January 1973, pp. 36–41. (Indeed, Ms. Stimpson's focus extends beyond "The Women's Movement" to include an attack on the entire corpus of Didion's published work.)

6. One example of such name-dropping seems almost to anticipate Wolfe's *Radical Chic:* "I saw the Senator in San Francisco," one patron remarks, "where I was with Mrs. Leonard Bernstein" (p. 87).

7. All references are to p. 52.

8. All references are to p. 27.

9. The technique at work here is similar to that which we find in a good deal of Hemingway's writing. "If a writer of prose knows enough about what he is writing about," Hemingway contends, "he may omit things. . . . The dignity of movement of an ice-berg is due to only one-eighth of it being above water." See *Death in the Afternoon* (New York, 1932), p. 192.

10. The original title of "On Morality" when that essay appeared in the *American Scholar*.

11. In *Play It as It Lays* the corpse of Maria's mother is torn apart by coyotes.

12. The title of this essay comes from the Beatles' "White Album." A record released in 1968, "it was almost the last time the four really worked together, and the fragmentation of the group, the collisions of spirit and explosions in different directions, are apparent in it. 'The White Album' was also a kind of catechism for Manson and his followers. The title of a song from it, 'Helter Skelter,' was written in blood on the refrigerator at the LaBianca house." See Martha Duffy's review of *The White Album*, *New York Review of Books*, August 16, 1979, p. 44.

13. Three weeks prior to the Tate-LaBianca murders, for example, Teddy Kennedy drove off the bridge at Chappaquiddick and Neil Armstrong stepped upon the surface of the moon. Many would argue that either of those events more emphatically signified the end of the 1960s than did the atrocities of the Manson Family.

14. Of course, the fragmented nature of Didion's narrative line is intentional. As Robert Towers points out in his review of *The White Album*, Didion "gives the impression of having refined" her personal neurosis "to the point where it vibrates in exquisite attunement to the larger craziness of the world she inhabits and observes" (*New York Times Book Review*, June 17, 1979, p. 1). In this instance, however, it seems to me that the author falls prey to what "new critics" used to call "the fallacy of imitative form."

15. She tells us that "disc jockeys telephoned my house and wanted to discuss (on the air) the incidence of 'filth' in the Haight-Ashbury, and acquaintances congratulated me on having finished the piece 'just in time,' because 'the whole fad's dead now, *fini, kaput*'" (*Slouching*, p. iv).

16. In contrast, Didion's inclusion of personal references in "The White Album" constitutes one of that essay's main virtues. (Its weaknesses lie elsewhere.)

Chapter Four

1. For a discussion of Didion as journalist, see Michael L. Johnson, *The New Journalism* (Lawrence, Kansas, 1971), pp. 96–100.

2. All references are to p. 14.

3. The resulting satirical effect is not unlike that of a line from Pope's *The Rape of the Lock*. Here, surveying her dressing table, Belinda finds: "Puffs, Powders, Patches, Bibles, Billet-doux."

4. In this connection one is reminded of a statement made by an extra working on the film version of *The Day of the Locust*. "For the first time in my life," he says, "I enjoy getting up to go to work. My work in Atlanta was so unsuitable it was unreal. The greatest feeling I have out here is being in touch with reality. This set and the people here and the people at the Figuero Hotel are realer to me than Atlanta ever was." See Tom Burke, "And it came to pass, just as Nathanael West told us: Hollywood collapsed and fell into this $88,000 hole on *The Day of the Locust*," *Esquire*, September 1974, p. 126. For a more extended discussion of Didion's views on Hollywood, see Chapter 9 below.

5. This is the title of one of the chapters of Kazin's *The Bright Book of Life* (Boston, 1973). In this chapter (pp. 209-41) its author discusses both the new journalism (Mailer, Baldwin, Capote, and others) and such recent historical fictions as William Styron's *The Confessions of Nat Turner*.

6. All references are to the version of this essay which appears in *The White Album* as "On the Mall" (pp. 180-86).

7. All references are to p. 20B. Although a revised version of this essay appears as part of the *White Album* sequence "Good Citizens" (pp. 92-95), I have chosen to remain with the original.

Chapter Five

1. In the preface of *Slouching Towards Bethlehem* Didion contends that *"writers are always selling somebody out"* (p. xiv).

2. *Existential Errands* (New York, 1972), p. 3.

3. In commenting on this phenomenon Christopher Lasch writes: "The mass media intensify narcissistic dreams of fame and glory, encouraging the common man to identify himself with the stars and to hate the 'herd,' and make it more and more difficult for him to accept the banality of everyday existence" (*The Culture of Narcissism* [New York: 1979], p. 21).

4. See "I'll Take Romance," *National Review*, September 24, 1963, p. 248.

5. Fifteen years later Wayne was once again stricken with cancer; however, this time the disease proved fatal. The Duke died on June 11, 1979.

6. The proposition that bosses make lousy lovers is one that Mrs. Brown has articulated in various talk-show appearances.

7. As is the case with many a lapsed believer, Joan Didion has rather conservative attitudes toward her former church. In this regard she is not dissimilar to a number of Roman Catholics who stopped attending Mass prior to Vatican II.

8. *The New Science of Politics* (Chicago, 1952), pp. 120, 121. For a more recent discussion of social millennialism, see Morris Dickstein's study of the 1960s—*The Gates of Eden* (New York, 1977).

9. This reference to the Trinity, coming, as it does, at the end of Didion's essay, is both structurally and thematically functional. Just as she has told us at the outset about Pike's earlier stance of theological reductionism—streamlining the Trinity—so too is she now alluding to that childlike faith in the occult which characterized the bishop's final years.

Chapter Six

1. In addition to the essays discussed here, the reader may also wish to look at four articles which Didion published in *Mademoiselle* early in her career: "Berkeley's Giant: The University of California," January 1960, pp. 88–90, 103, 105–107; "San Francisco Job Hunt," September 1960, pp. 128, 168–70; "New York: The Great Reprieve," February 1961, pp. 102–103, 147–48, 150–51; and "Washington, D.C.: 'Anything Can Happen Here,'" November 1962, pp. 132–35, 157–59, 162–63.

2. Some California essays are also discussed in Chapter 7. However, those essays—it seems to me—are part of Didion's effort to define the peculiar characteristics of the American West. In contrast, the writings discussed in the first section of this chapter deal with places which happen to be in California, but which—with the possible exception of San Simeon—could conceivably be located anywhere in America.

3. All references are to p. 16.

4. Nathanael West, *The Complete Works* (New York, 1975), p. 287.

5. See *The Hymnal of the Protestant Episcopal Church* (New York, 1940), #471. Since this hymnal was in use during Joan Didion's childhood, it is reasonable to assume that she was aware of Toplady's hymn.

6. The allusion here to Frost's "Stopping by Woods on a Snowy Evening" is appropriate. Like Didion, the speaker in Frost's poem is attracted by the prospect of security and isolation.

7. *Play It as It Lays* (New York, 1970), p. 172.

8. The naive reticence of this man is similar to the peculiarly North American innocence of Charlotte Douglas, protagonist of *A Book of Common Prayer*. (See Chapter 10 below.)

9. "Getting the Vegas Willies," *Esquire*, May 1977, p. 44. Although I have chosen not to discuss this essay in detail, it is another example of Didion's ability to evoke a sense of place.

10. At the time of Davidson's interview with her, the author was working on a novel set in Hawaii.

11. This sequence of essays contains—in addition to the author's discussion of James Jones—a shortened version of "A Problem of Making Connections" (see Chapter 1 above) and Didion's description of a Vietnam burial in Punchbowl (see Chapter 3 above). Also included here is an appreciation of the aristocratic ambience of Honolulu's Royal Hawaiian Hotel.

12. Robert E. Lee Prewitt, an Army bugler, is the protagonist of *From Here to Eternity*. Didion's reference to the Royal Hawaiian, however, is somewhat more complex. As a young man Jones had found that hotel to be a symbol of inaccessible elegance. But by 1973, it seemed to him to be "less formidably rich than he had left it in 1942, and it had occurred to him with considerable poignance that he was a man in his fifties who could walk into the Royal Hawaiian and buy whatever he wanted" ("Islands," p. 148).

13. In fact, Kakutani makes precisely this point at the outset of her article (p. 34). However, since the original version of the above chapter was written

some six and a half months before the publication of Kakutani's feature, I
have chosen to leave my own wording intact.

Chapter Seven

1. (New York, 1977), p. 231.
2. *Virgin Land* (Cambridge, Massachusetts, 1950), p. 45.
3. *The Machine in the Garden* (New York, 1964), pp. 43–44, 45.
4. *The Red Pony* (New York, 1938), p. 102.
5. *Hollywood in Fiction: Some Versions of the American Myth* (The Hague, 1969), p. 114.
6. *Tycoons and Locusts* (Carbondale, Illinois: 1973), p. 127. Elsewhere, Wells defines "the term *Southland*, a journalistic geologism," as "convenient shorthand for the sweep of coastal basins, ranges, and inland valleys that constitute southern California" (p. 10).
7. *Essays of Four Decades* (Chicago, 1968), p. 592.
8. In a December 1971 television interview broadcast by PBS: "Speaking Freely," with Edwin Newman.
9. And yet, Didion herself sees a similarity between these two regions. "The tension central to both the Southern and the Western experience," she writes, "is . . . [the] inability to distinguish between myth and reality." See "Notes from a Summer Reader," *National Review*, November 18, 1961, p. 342.
10. "Thinking About Western Thinking," *Esquire*, February 1976, p. 10. Subsequent page references in the text.
11. We must keep in mind that Didion is not endorsing Marion Faye's behavior, for her essay "On Morality" is, of course, a critique of the unfettered conscience.
12. Ever since the exile of our first parents to the *east* of Eden the movement of civilization has been westward. As the frontiers of paradise continued to be pushed further in that direction the new Eden, which was once all of America, eventually became only California. However, the attempt to return to Eden has always proved elusive. Our path is not barred by angels with flaming swords; it simply stops, beyond the last horizon, with a recognition that the quest for innocence is the ultimate vanity.
13. Indeed, Martha Duffy finds a substantial connection between Didion and Faulkner. She contends that Didion has "brought the Southern mentality west" and that "like Faulkner, Didion has an overwhelming awareness of human corruption and a sense of unfathomable doom." See Duffy's review of *Play It as It Lays*, *Time*, August 10, 1970, pp. 67, 68.
14. I suspect that even the syntax is important here. It is the Holy Land which resembles the Sacramento Valley, not the other way around.
15. Her description of the hop fields in the first paragraph of this story is a case in point: "They had started to strip the vines that week, and when they begin picking the hops, one knows that the summer is almost over in California" (p. 21).
16. We see the same sort of connection between a woman's love for her

father and her rootedness in place in the character of Lily Knight McClellan in *Run River*. Both Messrs. Cavanaugh and Knight consider their respective daughters to be superior to the children of the more recent Valley residents and both men try to impress upon those daughters a sense of their pioneer heritage. After telling her about her nineteenth-century forebears, Laura's father says "harshly": "You're the heiress to that entire century . . . and you'd better be damn proud of it" (p. 23). Similarly, when Lily says to her father, "Sometimes I think this whole valley belongs to me," Walter Knight responds "sharply," "It does, you hear me? . . . We made it" (*Run River*, p. 85).

17. In addition to the previously cited quotation from *Peck's 1837 New Guide to the West*, the following passage from Robert Lowell's "Man and Wife" appears on the fly-leaf of *Run River*:

> All night I've held your hand,
> as if you had
> a fourth time faced the kingdom of the mad—
> its hackneyed speech, its homicidal eye—
> and dragged me home alive . . .

18. *Run River* (New York, 1963). Page references appear in the text.

19. Indeed, we have here what Norman Friedman calls "multiple selective omniscience." "Here the reader ostensibly listens to no one; the story comes directly through the minds of the characters as it leaves its mark there. As a result, the tendency is almost wholly in the direction of scene, both inside the mind and externally with speech and action; and narrative summary, if it appears at all, is either supplied unobtrusively by the author by way of 'stage direction' or emerges through the thoughts and words of the characters themselves." See "Point of View in Fiction: The Development of a Critical Concept," *PMLA* 70 (1955): 1176.

20. Similarly, there is a left-wing Jewish girl friend—Naomi Kahn—in Everett's past. See pp. 167–68.

21. In another context Didion has written that when she lived in New York she was "most comfortable in the company of Southerners. They seemed to me to be in New York as I was, on some indefinitely extended leave from wherever they belonged . . . , temporary exiles who always knew when the flights left for New Orleans or Memphis or Richmond or, in my case, California" (*Slouching*, p. 230).

22. This particular story comes from Didion's own family history. See "Thinking About Western Thinking," p. 10.

23. Although hardly a comic novel, *Run River* is far from being humorless. Certainly, Guy Davenport overstates his case when he says of Didion's book: "All humor, all irony have been pared away." See "Midas' Grandchildren," *National Review*, May 7, 1963, p. 371. (Perhaps in 1963 *National Review* did not consider humor at the expense of conservatives to be funny.)

24. One suspects that if Channing were aware of these traditions that he would file them away in his mind under *"Growers, Social Eccentricities of."*

Indeed, an incident involving John McClellan and his daughter Martha is filed under this very category. Here, McClellan identifies Ryder as "that fellow from Mississippi." When his daughter corrects him, the rancher replies: "Mississippi, Tennessee, what's the difference. . . . It's all Del Paso Heights to me" (p. 125). ("Del Paso Heights was a district north of Sacramento noted for its large Negro population and its high incidence of social disorders" [p. 125].)

25. An even more ludicrous conflict of cultures occurs when Channing introduces Martha to a Cadillac dealer who claims to have met her father at the Sacramento Rotary. When she indicates that her father has been dead since 1944, the dealer admits, "I wasn't here in 1944" (p. 212). But later, as he is leaving, he says to *Martha*, "Remember me to your dad Marty. . . . *Hasta Luego* for now" (p. 213).

26. *Advertisements for Myself* (New York, 1959), p. 466.

27. Indeed, in her review of *A Book of Common Prayer*, Joyce Carol Oates identifies Martha as the heroine of *Run River*. See *New York Times Book Review*, April 3, 1977, p. 34.

28. This parade is supposed to have taken place exactly one year after the author had witnessed those California state legislators in their green hats. Both the spectacle in the legislature and the parade in *Run River* are quaint vestiges of the small-town California of Didion's youth.

29. One wonders whether the cherry tree here is meant to have Chekhovian implications. Later on in the novel Knight McClellan accuses his grandmother, Edith Knight, of reminding him "more every day of something out of *The Cherry Orchard*" (p. 248).

30. Of course, Lily's mother survives Walter Knight; however, she is presented throughout the novel as a rather vacuous person who spends much of her time watching the Dodgers on television. (Indeed, this pastime itself may be significant; for the Los Angeles Dodgers are in many ways emblematic of the postwar boom. Transplanted easterners, they came west from Brooklyn to settle in Chavez Ravine as part of a real-estate transaction.)

31. Lily is even more deeply alienated from her son Knight. In a fit of pique at his father, the boy snarls, "*Last Saturday night . . .* your wife was shacked up at Lake Tahoe. . . . They call her Lily Knight, not McClellan, *Knight*. Like she was never married at all" (p. 253).

Chapter Eight

1. *Telling Stories*, p. 10. This book is a collection of Didion's three stories from the 1960s along with an introductory chapter in which the author discusses her views on and experience with short fiction. Since *Telling Stories* was privately published by the Bancroft Library at Berkeley and is thus not widely accessible, all references to the stories themselves will be to the magazines in which they originally appeared.

2. This concept, which is borrowed from Allen Tate, is discussed more fully in the next chapter.

3. Revised edition (New York, 1966). See especially Chapter Eight: "*Clarissa* in America: Toward Marjorie Morningstar" (pp. 217–58). I am greatly indebted to a friend and colleague, Mr. Wayne Batten, for providing me with a number of fascinating insights into Professor Fiedler's thesis.

4. Her pantheon of Dionysian lovers includes Miller Hardin in "The Welfare Island Ferry"; Ward in "When Did Music Come This Way . . . ?"; Ryder Channing in *Run River*; and Warren Bogart in *A Book of Common Prayer*; whereas Charlie Sloane in "Coming Home" and the narrator's husband in "When Did Music Come This Way . . . ?" are merely petty sadists who never approach mythic status. (Carter Lang in *Play It as It Lays* could conceivably be placed in either category.) Finally, Didion's benign or Apollonian prototypes include Everett McClellan in *Run River*, Les Goodwin in *Play It as It Lays*, and Leonard Douglas in *A Book of Common Prayer*. (Perhaps Henry Taylor in "The Welfare Island Ferry" would also have been such a figure had his character been more fully developed.)

5. If this troubled relationship between a western woman and a southern man echoes the story of Lily McClellan and Ryder Channing in *Run River*, it also anticipates that of Charlotte Douglas and Warren Bogart in *A Book of Common Prayer*.

6. When Miller introduces Louisa to his friends, he says, "This is Miss Louisa Patterson Pool. . . . Never mind where I found her. Hasn't she got nice legs" (p. 82). In a similar vein but with considerably less wit, Johnny Waters in *Play It as It Lays* says of Maria, "This is Myra. . . . I just found her some place" (p. 152).

7. Loss of innocence through a vicarious and enigmatic encounter with adult sexuality is a common theme in literature, and can be found in such diverse stories as James Joyce's "Araby" and Sherwood Anderson's "I Want to Know Why."

8. Not only are her cousin, aunt, and husband lost to her, but the narrator also tells us that she sees her parents only once a year: "They seem older and to prefer talking to the children than to me" (p. 61).

Chapter Nine

1. Quoted in James F. Light, *Nathanael West: An Interpretative Study*, second edition (Evanston, Illinois: 1971), p. 168. In making much the same point about *Play It as It Lays* Wilfrid Sheed writes that Didion's Hollywood is "not the fiction Hollywood where dreams are shattered on casting couches, but a real professional shop town where actual movies are made. . . . [Maria's] problems as a starlet, producer's wife, etc. are not make-problems, but the distillations of a talented reporter's observation of Hollywood fever." See Sheed's review of *Play It as It Lays*, *Life*, July 31, 1970, p. 13.

2. *The Loved One* (Boston, 1948), p. 122.

3. *The Collected Stories* (New York, 1950), p. 724.

4. An example of the bad feelings between Didion and Kauffmann can be found in an exchange of letters between them shortly after the original

publication of "In Hollywood" (see *New York Review of Books*, April 19, 1973, p. 43); while we need only turn to Didion's discussion of Simon in "Monster" (p. 155) to see what she thinks of that critic. Finally, one can find an account of Didion's relations with Ms. Kael in John Gregory Dunne's essay "Pauline" (*Quintana and Friends*, pp. 150–57).

5. *New York Review of Books*, August 16, 1979, pp. 18–19.

6. "I can't get that monster out of my mind" is a line from a horror movie. ("It is a useful line," Didion writes, "and one that frequently occurs to me when I catch the tone in which a great many people write or talk about Hollywood," *Slouching*, pp. 149–50.)

7. The only substantive disagreement between these essays is that "In Hollywood" gives greater credence to the continuing dominance of the major studios than does "Monster."

8. "Actually it takes a fairly romantic sensibility," Didion continues, "to discern why the Garden of Allah should have been a more insidious ambience than the Algonquin, or why the Thalberg Building, and Metro-Goldwyn-Mayer, should have been more morally debilitating than the Graybar Building, and *Vanity Fair*" (p. 150).

9. In "Why I Write" Didion says that her technical intention in *Play It as It Lays* was to write "a book in which anything that happened would happen off the page, a 'white' book to which the reader would have to bring his or her own bad dreams" (p. 98).

10. *National Review*, August 25, 1970, p. 903.

11. *Bright Book of Life*, p. 195.

12. *Play It as It Lays* (New York, 1970). Page references in text.

13. This device is used even more prominently in the movie version of *Play It as It Lays*. In one particularly memorable scene Maria is watching a television talk show in which Carter is showing and discussing the film *Maria*. Thus we are seeing something which—in terms of Didion's story—purports to be *cinéma vérité*; but which—from our perspective—is a film within a TV show within a film.

14. At one point the protagonist of Percy's novel says, "Nowadays when a person lives somewhere, in a neighborhood, the place is not certified for him. . . . But if he sees a movie which shows his very neighborhood, it becomes possible for him to live, for a time at least, as a person who is Somewhere and not Anywhere" (New York, 1961, p. 63).

15. *The Prisoner of Sex* (Boston, 1971), pp. 140–41.

16. The theme of depersonalization is emphasized by the fact that Johnny Waters refers to Maria as "Myra." (Indeed, in this respect, he is somewhat reminiscent of the Cadillac dealer in *Run River* who keeps calling Martha McClellan "Marty.")

17. We learn that Ivan used to call Maria in the middle of the night. "'How much do you want it,' he used to say. 'Tell me what you'd do to get it from me'" (p. 71). These lines, of course, echo Ward's interrogation of Inez in "When Did Music Come This Way . . . ?"

18. Ironically, it is Maria's love for Kate—and her fear that Carter will

otherwise prevent her from seeing Kate—which causes Maria to agree to the abortion.

19. See "Nothingness and Beyond: Joan Didion's *Play It as It Lays*," *Critique: Studies in Modern Fiction* 16 (1974): 71.

20. Late in the novel Maria tells Carter about a man who left his home in a trailer camp to search for God in the desert. Instead of talking to God, he was bitten by a rattlesnake. "Do you think God answered," Maria inquires. "Or don't you?" (p. 204).

21. *The Myth of Sisyphus*, tr. Justin O'Brien (London, 1955), p. 11. Geherin also invokes Camus; however, he goes on to interpret Maria's response to the dilemma of life as a positive one.

22. In the film version of *Play It as It Lays* BZ tells Maria that his grandfather—a wealthy Jew—committed suicide and that that man's son (BZ's father) once studied for the Roman Catholic priesthood, only to die later of acute alcoholism.

23. Note the similarity between Todd's reference to Hamlet and Maria's to Iago. See *The Floating Opera*, rev. ed. (Garden City, New York, 1967), pp. 250, 251. I wish to thank a former colleague—Mr. Gary Cohen—for pointing out the above parallel between *Play It as It Lays* and *The Floating Opera*.

24. *Complete Plays with Prefaces* (New York, 1962), II, 7. A more immediate source for Maria's exchange with BZ can be found, however, in Didion's own "Los Angeles Notebook." Here, the author is in a Southern California piano bar surrounded by meaningless and inane conversation. (There is an argument, for example, between a drunk who requests "The Sweetheart of Sigma Chi" and the piano player, who boasts of his degree in music education.) Didion goes to the telephone and calls a friend in New York: "'Where are you?' he says. 'In a piano bar in Encino,' I say. 'Why?' he says. 'Why not, I say" (*Slouching*, p. 224).

25. *Hemingway: The Writer as Artist* (Princeton, New Jersey, 1952), p. 124.

Chapter Ten

1. *A Book of Common Prayer* (New York, 1977). Page references in the text.

2. Even Marin's name may be significant. Marin County, California is in the San Francisco Bay area, a region where the Black Panthers were founded and where Randolph Hearst tried to ransom his daughter from the SLA with a massive distribution of food to the poor.

3. "The Epistemology of *The Good Soldier*," *Sewanee Review* 69 (Spring 1961): 225.

4. Omniscient point of view appears to have made something of a comeback in recent years. (One thinks of the works of British novelists like John Fowles and Margaret Drabble and, in this country, of Truman Capote's *In Cold Blood*.) But the *general* trend toward limited point of view seems still to be very much with us.

5. Grace herself recognizes the limitations imposed by language on one's attempt to comprehend and communicate experience: "Everything here changes," she says, "but nothing appears to. There is . . . only the amniotic stillness in which transformations are constant. As elsewhere, certain phases in these transformations are called by certain names ('Oldsmobile,' say, and 'rust'), but the emotional field of such names tends to weaken as one leaves the temperate zones. At the equator the names are noticeably arbitrary. A banana palm is no more or less 'alive' than its rot" (p. 155).

6. "Joan Didion and Her Characters," *Commentary*, July 1977, pp. 62–63.

7. *The Nature of Narrative* (New York, 1966), p. 261.

8. Technically, *Absalom, Absalom!* is narrated from a selectively omniscient third-person perspective; however, Shreve and Quentin are the most important *centers of consciousness* in Faulkner's novel.

9. There are critics who disagree with this statement, who argue that Grace is—in fact—an obtuse narrator. See, for example, Peter S. Prescott's review of *A Book of Common Prayer*, *Newsweek*, March 21, 1977, p. 81; and Diane Johnson's "Hard Hit Women," *New York Review of Books*, April 28, 1977, p. 6.

10. I am using the term "Protestant" in its cultural sense. Of course, the Anglican Communion has always claimed that sacramentally it is a Catholic body.

11. Ransom makes this point in a number of places, but most insistently in *God Without Thunder* (New York, 1930).

12. It may be that Grace's failure to know *the* truth is finally less significant than her ability to communicate *a* truth. Perhaps Didion's use of the indefinite article in her title is meant to suggest that Grace has written a private liturgy. If we as readers see some truth in that liturgy, it becomes to that extent "common." In any event, what we have here is not a Christian vision but a decidedly humanistic one.

13. Others have noted the irony in Grace's name and condition. In addition to Prescott's review, see Walter Sullivan's "Fiction Chronicle," *Sewanee Review* 86 (Winter 1978): 154.

14. R. Z. Sheppard, however, goes so far as to see Didion's novel as a modern version of James's *Portrait of a Lady*. See *Time*, March 28, 1977, p. 87.

15. Warren seems to be able to work his will on people in much the same way as the unnamed friend whom Didion describes in her essay on "Emotional Blackmail." When Warren is trying to lure Charlotte away from Leonard, for example, he says, "I want you to see Porter with me. Porter is dying. Porter wants to see you. Do this one thing for me." And a bit later: "If you won't do it for me you'll do it for Porter. Or you're a worse human being than even I think" (p. 102).

16. In *Run River* we read that Ryder Channing "had once told Everett that wherever he was he made a point of getting a guest card to the best country club" (p. 151).

17. The Alexander Woolcott parallel was suggested to me by Warren French.

18. In a sense, the separation of Charlotte and Marin is as unavoidable as the parting of Frederick Henry and Catherine Barkley at the end of *A Farewell to Arms*. Try as one might, it is not always possible to overcome the force of nature and circumstance.

19. This technique of indirection is similar to the one which Hugh Kenner contends that Faulkner uses in telling Caddy's story in *The Sound and the Fury*. For Kenner's discussion of Faulkner, see *A Homemade World* (New York, 1975), pp. 194–221.

20. In *The American Adam* (Chicago, 1955) R. W. B. Lewis describes the paradigmatic nineteenth-century American as "a figure of heroic innocence and vast potentialities poised at the start of a new history" (p. 1). The modern world, however, regards such innocence as more of a liability than an asset.

Chapter Eleven

1. *Dubliners* (New York, 1961), p. 210.

2. "When Did Music Come This Way . . . ?," p. 54.

3. "(She later recalled that at sixteen she had considered suicide with a length of garden hose and her mother's station wagon, but managed to abandon this version of herself in favor of the other)" (p. 83).

4. For further associations between this song and marital discord, see "On the Morning after the Sixties," *Album*, p. 205.

5. These latter two novels also feature a counterpoint of more immediate music. In *Play It as It Lays* Maria is assaulted, while riding in Johnny Waters's car, by the cacophonous sounds of "Midnight Hour" (p. 150), and later—when in Vegas—by those of "Spinning Wheel" and "Son of a Preacher Man" (p. 170). Then, at the end of the novel, BZ commits suicide against the background of a country-western formulation of the "play it as it lays" philosophy—Roger Miller's "King of the Road" (p. 212). Finally, in *A Book of Common Prayer*, we find Warren commandeering the piano in Morgan Fayard's home to teach his evening's companion to play: "*May the fish get legs and the cows lay eggs—If ever I cease to love—May the moon be turned to green cream cheese—If ever I cease to love—May the—*" (p. 171).

6. "Novels and Nothingness," *American Scholar* 40 (Winter 1970–71): 174.

7. *Bright Book of Life*, p. 195.

8. "Divided Selves," *New York Review of Books*, October 22, 1970, p. 42.

9. See Kazin's "Portrait of a Professional," p. 113.

10. Lore Segal, *New York Times Book Review*, August 9, 1970, p. 18.

11. The subtitle of Norman Mailer's nonfiction novel *The Armies of the Night* is *History as Novel* [/] *The Novel as History*.

12. A particularly egregious example of such condescension can be found in *Run River*. Here Lily, returning by Greyhound bus from her abortion in

San Francisco, encounters two ingenuous representatives of the lower middle class. One is a sailor who sits on his duffel bag while reading a comic book and munching a Milky Way. The other is a woman who talks incessantly about her daughter Sue Ann. (A drive-in waitress who looks like Rita Hayworth, Sue Ann has a six-year-old son named Billy Jack and is currently pursuing happiness with an up-and-coming vacuum cleaner salesman.) "There would be nothing ambiguous about Sue Ann's responses," Lily thinks, "nothing ambivalent about her wants. . . . Sue Ann's problems, unlike her own, offered the compression, the foreshortening of art" (p. 178).

Selected Bibliography

PRIMARY SOURCES

1. Books

A Book of Common Prayer. New York: Simon and Schuster, 1977.
Play It as It Lays. New York: Farrar, Straus, and Giroux, 1970.
Run River. New York: Ivan Obolensky, 1963.
Slouching Towards Bethlehem. New York: Farrar, Straus, and Giroux, 1968.
Telling Stories. Berkeley, California: Bancroft Library, 1978.
The White Album. New York: Simon and Schuster, 1979.

2. Uncollected Prose

For a relatively complete and reasonably accurate listing of Joan Didion's uncollected prose through March 1, 1977, see Fred Rue Jacobs, *Joan Didion—Bibliography*.
"Getting the Vegas Willies." *Esquire*, May 1977, pp. 32, 44–46.
"Letter from 'Manhattan.'" *New York Review of Books*, August 16, 1979, pp. 18–19.
Review of *Falconer*, by John Cheever. *New York Times Book Review*, March 6, 1977, pp. 1, 22, 24.
Review of *Sleepless Nights*, by Elizabeth Hardwick. *New York Times Book Review*, April 29, 1979, pp. 1, 60.

SECONDARY SOURCES

1. Bibliography

JACOBS, FRED RUE. *Joan Didion—Bibliography*. Keene, California: Loop Press, 1977. A useful, though flawed, bibliography of both primary and secondary sources. Contains numerous printing errors—particularly within its listing of secondary material.

2. Biography and General Criticism

BRAUDY, SUSAN. "A Day in the Life of Joan Didion," *Ms.*, February 1977, pp. 65–68, 108–109. An account of an interview with Didion, complete with Ms. Braudy's own feminist commentary.

172

DAVIDSON, SARA. "A Visit with Joan Didion," *New York Times Book Review*, April 3, 1977, pp. 1, 35–38. An excellent interview with Didion shortly after the publication of *A Book of Common Prayer.*

DIAMONSTEIN, BARBARALEE. *Open Secrets: Ninety-four Women in Touch with Our Time.* New York: Viking Press, 1970, pp. 103–106. Didion is one of ninety-four women to respond briefly to some general and rather superficial questions.

KAKUTANI, MICHIKO. "Joan Didion: Staking Out California," *New York Times Magazine*, June 10, 1979, pp. 34, 36, 38, 40, 44, 46, 48, 50. An informative biographical feature which appeared just prior to the publication of *The White Album.*

KAZIN, ALFRED. *Bright Book of Life: American Novelists and Storytellers from Hemingway to Mailer.* Boston: Little, Brown and Company, 1973, pp. 189–98. A short critical account of Didion's career through *Play It as It Lays.*

———. "Joan Didion: Portrait of a Professional," *Harper's*, December 1971, pp. 112–14, 116, 118, 120–22. Biographical and critical essay, part of which later appeared in *Bright Book of Life.*

NEWTON, JUDITH. "Joan Didion, 1972." *Female Studies VI: Closer to the Ground.* Ed. by Nancy Hoffman, Cynthia Secor, and Adrian Tinsley. Old Westbury, New York: Feminist Press, 1972, pp. 110–15. An attempt to demonstrate inconsistencies between the political attitudes expressed in "The Women's Movement" and Didion's own literary practice.

STIMPSON, CATHERINE. "The Case of Miss Joan Didion," *Ms.*, January 1973, pp. 36–41. Feminist attack on Didion as "a curious creature, whose sense of literature and life is common, disappointingly conventional, and always problematical."

3. On *A Book of Common Prayer*

OATES, JOYCE CAROL. "A Taut Novel of Disorder," *New York Times Book Review*, April 3, 1977, pp. 1, 34–35. Didion "has been an articulate witness to the most stubborn and intractable truths of our time, a memorable voice . . . , always in control."

PRESCOTT, PETER S. "Didion's Grace," *Newsweek*, March 21, 1977, p. 81. Compares Didion with Joseph Conrad and Graham Greene.

RAPHAEL, FREDERICK. "Grace Under Pressure," *Saturday Review*, March 5, 1977, pp. 23–25. One senses in Didion "the quick desire for something more noble, more tender, and more enduring than crass contemporary 'realism.'"

ROMANO, JOHN. "Joan Didion and Her Characters," *Commentary*, July 1977, pp. 61–63. Sees Grace's story as "an allegory of the progress of the liberal, humanistic intelligence in the last twenty years."

SHEPPARD, R. Z. "The Imagination of Disaster," *Time*, March 28, 1977, p. 87. "Joan Didion has produced a remarkable modern variation on Henry James's *The Portrait of a Lady.*"

4. On *Play It as It Lays*

DAVENPORT, GUY. "On the Edge of Being," *National Review*, August 25, 1970, pp. 903–904. "Miss Didion has evolved for this tragedy a mode of writing that is somehow both pitiless in its gaze and compassionate in its concern."

DUFFY, MARTHA. "Survivor's Report," *Time*, August 10, 1970, pp. 67–68. Views *Play It as It Lays* within the context of Didion's previous career. Draws parallel between Didion and Faulkner.

GEHERIN, DAVID J. "Nothingness and Beyond: Joan Didion's *Play It as It Lays*," *Critique: Studies in Modern Fiction* 16 (1974): 64–78. Discusses novel within the context of Camus' philosophy. Sees Maria as having pushed beyond nothingness to a limited affirmation of meaning.

JONES, D. A. N. "Divided Selves," *New York Review of Books*, October 22, 1970, pp. 38–42. Finds in the novel "a certain exhiliration, as when we appreciate a harmonious and well-proportioned painting of some cruelly martyred saint in whom we do not believe."

LEONARD, JOHN. "The Cities of the Desert, the Desert of the Mind," *New York Times*, July 21, 1970, p. 33. "There hasn't been another American writer of Joan Didion's quality since Nathanael West. . . . [Her vision in *Play It as It Lays* is] as bleak and precise as Eliot's in *The Waste Land*."

SCHORER, MARK. "Novels and Nothingness," *American Scholar* 40 (Winter 1970–71): 169, 170, 172, 174. When reading this novel "one thinks of the great *performers* in ballet, opera, circuses." It is "a triumph not of insight as such but of style."

5. On *Run River*

DAVENPORT, GUY. "Midas' Grandchildren," *National Review*, May 7, 1963, p. 371. Dialogue between an imaginary "critic" and "reader." Makes good interpretative points about the novel, but is perplexing in its point of view.

"Lily of the Valley," *Times Literary Supplement*, January 30, 1964, p. 92. Sees *Run River* as "a beautifully told first novel. Written in prose both witty and imaginative, it has too a high level of intelligence."

MAUER, ROBERT. "Lifeless by the Fruitful Sacramento," *New York Herald Tribune Book Review*, May 12, 1963, p. 10. Argues that, despite her technical proficiency, Didion—unlike Philip Roth—does not see life "as possessing a tang."

6. On *Slouching Towards Bethlehem*

JOHNSON, MICHAEL. *The New Journalism*. Lawrence: University of Kansas Press, 1971, pp. 96–100. Compares Didion's journalistic writings with those of Truman Capote, Tom Wolfe, and Dan Wakefield.

"Somewhere Else," *Times Literary Supplement*, February 12, 1970, p. 153.

"Between her provincial roots and the two cosmopolitan coasts, between her Happy Valley and urban paranoia, Joan Didion wanders, slightly dazed but acutely observant."

WAKEFIELD, DAN. Review of *Slouching Towards Bethlehem*. *New York Times Book Review*, July 21, 1968, p. 8. *Slouching* is "a rich display of some of the best prose written today in this country."

7. On *The White Album*

CLEMONS, WALTER. "Didion Country." *Newsweek*, June 25, 1979, pp. 84–85. Sees Didion as a better journalist than novelist. "*The White Album* is her best book since *Slouching Towards Bethlehem*."

DUFFY, MARTHA. "Pictures from an Expedition," *New York Review of Books*, August 16, 1979, pp. 43–44. "The essays in *The White Album* . . . in some ways . . . are better than her fiction, because in her novels she submerges her own voice."

SIMON, JOHN. "De Tenuissimis Clamavi." *National Review*, October 12, 1979, pp. 1311–1312. "After reading such outpourings of hypersensitivity in quotidian conflict, one feels positively relieved to be an insensitive clod."

TOWERS, ROBERT. "The Decline and Fall of the 60's," *New York Times Book Review*, pp. 1, 30. Didion's "is a voice like no other in contemporary journalism."

Index

DATE DUE

DEMCO 38-297